The
Whole-Brain
Child

The Whole-Brain Child

12 Revolutionary Strategies to
Nurture Your Child's Developing Mind

DANIEL J. SIEGEL, M.D., *and*
TINA PAYNE BRYSON, PH.D.

DELACORTE PRESS
New York

For Maddi and Alex: Thank you both for all you've taught me over these years and for the privilege of being your dad; and for Caroline, for the love and our journey together —DJS

For the men in my life: my husband, Scott, and our three boys. You fill every day with fun, adventure, love, and meaning. —TPB

All identifying details, including names, have been changed except for those pertaining to the authors' family members. This book is not intended as a substitute for advice from a trained professional.

Copyright © 2011 by Mind Your Brain, Inc., and Bryson Creative Productions, Inc.

Published in the United States by Delacorte Press, an imprint of The Random House Publishing Group, a division of Random House, Inc., New York.

DELACORTE and colophon are registered trademarks of Random House, Inc.

LIBRARY OF CONGRESS CATALOGING-IN-PUBLICATION DATA
Siegel, Daniel J.
   The whole-brain child : 12 revolutionary strategies to nurture your child's developing mind / Daniel J. Siegel, Tina Payne Bryson.
      p.   cm.
Includes index.
ISBN 978-0-553-80791-2—ISBN 978-0-553-90725-4 (e-book)
1. Parenting.   2. Child development.   3. Child rearing.
I. Bryson, Tina Payne.   II. Title.
HQ755.8.S53123 2011
649'.1019—dc22   2010052988

Illustrations by Tuesday Mourning

Printed in the United States of America on acid-free paper

9 8 7 6 5 4 3 2 1

Book design by Mary A. Wirth

Contents

Survive *and* Thrive

You've had those days, right? When the sleep deprivation, the muddy cleats, the peanut butter on the new jacket, the homework battles, the Play-Doh in your computer keyboard, and the refrains of "She started it!" leave you counting the minutes until bedtime. On these days, when you (again?!!) have to pry a raisin from a nostril, it seems like the most you can hope for is to *survive*.

However, when it comes to your children, you're aiming a lot higher than mere survival. Of course you want to get through those difficult tantrum-in-the-restaurant moments. But whether you're a parent or other committed caregiver in a child's life, your ultimate goal is to raise kids in a way that lets them *thrive*. You want them to enjoy meaningful relationships, be caring and compassionate, do well in school, work hard and be responsible, and feel good about who they are.

Survive. Thrive.

We've met with thousands of parents over the years. When we ask them what matters most to them, versions of these two goals almost always top the list. They want to survive difficult parenting moments, and they want their kids and their family to thrive. As parents ourselves, we share these same goals for our own families.

In our nobler, calmer, saner moments, we care about nurturing our kids' minds, increasing their sense of wonder, and helping them reach their potential in all aspects of life. But in the more frantic, stressful, bribe-the-toddler-into-the-car-seat-so-we-can-rush-to-the-soccer-game moments, sometimes all we can hope for is to avoid yelling or hearing someone say, "You're so mean!"

Take a moment and ask yourself: What do you really want for your children? What qualities do you hope they develop and take into their adult lives? Most likely you want them to be happy, independent, and successful. You want them to enjoy fulfilling relationships and live a life full of meaning and purpose. Now think about what percentage of your time you spend intentionally developing these qualities in your children. If you're like most parents, you worry that you spend too much time just trying to get through the day (and sometimes the next five minutes) and not enough time creating experiences that help your children thrive, both today and in the future.

You might even measure yourself against some sort of perfect parent who never struggles to survive, who seemingly spends every waking second helping her children thrive. You know, the PTA president who cooks organic, well-balanced meals while reading to her kids in Latin about the importance of helping others, then escorts them to the art museum in the hybrid that plays classical music and mists lavender aromatherapy through the air-conditioning vents. None of us can match up to this imaginary superparent. Especially when we feel like a large percentage of our days are spent in full-blown survival mode, where we find ourselves wild-eyed and red-faced at the end of a birthday party, shouting, "If there's one more argument over that bow and arrow, nobody's getting *any* presents!"

If any of this sounds familiar, we've got great news for you: *the moments you are just trying to survive are actually opportunities to help your child thrive.* At times you may feel that the loving, important moments (like having a meaningful conversation about compassion or character) are separate from the parenting challenges (like fighting another homework battle or dealing with another meltdown). But they are not separate at all. When your child is disrespectful and talks back to you, when you are asked to come in for a meeting with the principal, when you find crayon scribbles all over your wall: these are survive moments, no question about it. But at the same time, they are opportunities—even gifts—because a survive moment is *also* a thrive moment, where the important, meaningful work of parenting takes place.

For example, think about a situation you often just try to get through. Maybe when your kids are fighting with each other for the third time within three minutes. (Not too hard to imagine, is it?) Instead of just breaking up the fight and sending the sparring siblings to different rooms, you can use the argument as an opportunity for teaching: about reflective listening and hearing another person's point of view; about clearly and respectfully communicating your own desires; about compromise, sacrifice, negotiation, and forgiveness. We know: it sounds hard to imagine in the heat of the moment. But when you understand a little bit about your children's emotional needs and mental states, you can create this kind of positive outcome—even without United Nations peacekeeping forces.

There's nothing wrong with separating your kids when they're fighting. It's a good survival technique, and in certain situations it may be the best solution. But often we can do better than just ending the conflict and noise. We can transform the experience into one that develops not only each child's brain but also her relationship skills and her character. Over time, the siblings will each continue to grow and become more proficient at handling conflict without parental guidance. This will be just one of the many ways you can help them thrive.

What's great about this survive-and-thrive approach is that you don't have to try to carve out special time to help your children thrive. You can use *all* of the interactions you share—the stressful, angry ones as well as the miraculous, adorable ones—as opportunities to help them become the responsible, caring, capable people you want them to be. That's what this book is about: using those everyday moments with your kids to help them reach their true potential. The following pages offer an antidote to parenting and academic approaches that overemphasize achievement and perfection at any cost. We'll focus instead on ways you can help your kids be more themselves, more at ease in the world, filled with more resilience and strength. How do you do that? Our answer is simple: you need to understand some basics about the young brain that you are helping to grow and develop. That's what *The Whole-Brain Child* is all about.

How to Use This Book

Whether you're a parent, grandparent, teacher, therapist, or other significant caregiver in a child's life, we've written this book for you. We'll use the word "parent" throughout, but we're talking to anyone doing the crucial work of raising, supporting, and nurturing kids. Our goal is to teach you how to use your everyday interactions as opportunities to help you and the children you care for both survive and thrive. Though much of what you'll read can be creatively tailored for teens—in fact, we plan to write a follow-up that does just that—this book focuses on the years from birth to twelve, centering especially on toddlers, school-age kids, and preteens.

In the following pages we explain the whole-brain perspective and give you a variety of strategies to help your children be happier, healthier, and more fully themselves. The first chapter presents the concept of parenting with the brain in mind and introduces the simple and powerful concept at the heart of the whole-brain approach, integration. Chapter 2 focuses on helping a child's left brain and right brain work together so the child can be connected to both his logical and emotional selves. Chapter 3 emphasizes the importance of connecting the instinctual "downstairs brain" with the more thoughtful "upstairs brain," which is responsible for decision making, personal insight, empathy, and morality. Chapter 4 explains how you can help your child deal with painful moments from the past by shining the light of understanding on them, so they can be addressed in a gentle, conscious, and intentional way. Chapter 5 helps you teach your kids that they have the capacity to pause and reflect on their own state of mind.

When they can do that, they can make choices that give them control over how they feel and how they respond to their world. Chapter 6 highlights ways you can teach your children about the happiness and fulfillment that result from being connected to others, while still maintaining a unique identity.

A clear understanding of these different aspects of the whole-brain approach will allow you to view parenting in a whole new way. As parents, we are wired to try to save our children from any harm and hurt, but ultimately we can't. They'll fall down, they'll get their feelings hurt, and they'll get scared and sad and angry. Actually, it's often these difficult experiences that allow them to grow and learn about the world. Rather than trying to shelter our children from life's inevitable difficulties, we can help them integrate those experiences into their understanding of the world and learn from them. How our kids make sense of their young lives is not only about what happens to them but also about how their parents, teachers, and other caregivers respond.

With that in mind, one of our primary goals has been to make *The Whole-Brain Child* as helpful as possible by giving you these specific tools to make your parenting easier and your relationships with your children more meaningful. That's one reason roughly half of every chapter is devoted to "What You Can Do" sections, where we provide practical suggestions and examples of how you can apply the scientific concepts from that chapter.

Also, at the end of each chapter you'll find two sections designed to help you readily implement your new knowledge. The first is "Whole-Brain Kids," written to help you teach your children the basics of what we've covered in that particular chapter. It might seem strange to talk to young children about the brain. It *is* brain science, after all. But we've found that even small children—as young as four or five—really can understand some important basics about the way the brain works, and in turn understand themselves and their behavior and feelings in new and more insightful ways. This knowledge can be very powerful for the child, as well as the parent who is trying to teach, to discipline, and to love in ways that feel good to both of them. We've written the

"Whole-Brain Kids" sections with a school-age audience in mind, but feel free to adapt the information as you read aloud, so that it's developmentally appropriate for your child.

The other section at the end of each chapter is called "Integrating Ourselves." Whereas most of the book focuses on the inner life of your child and the connection between the two of you, here we'll help you apply each chapter's concepts to your own life and relationships. As children develop, their brains "mirror" their parent's brain. In other words, the parent's own growth and development, or lack of those, impact the child's brain. As parents become more aware and emotionally healthy, their children reap the rewards and move toward health as well. That means that integrating and cultivating your own brain is one of the most loving and generous gifts you can give your children.

Another tool we hope you'll find helpful is the "Ages and Stages" chart at the end of the book, where we offer a simple summary of how the book's ideas can be implemented according to the age of your child. Each chapter of the book is designed to help you put its ideas immediately into practice, with multiple suggestions appearing throughout to address various ages and stages of childhood development. But to make it easier for parents, this final reference section will categorize the book's suggestions according to age and development. If you're the mother of a toddler, for example, you can quickly find a reminder of what you can do to enhance integration between your child's left and right brain. Then, as your toddler grows, you can come back to the book at each age and view a list of the examples and suggestions most relevant to your child's new stage.

Additionally, just before the "Ages and Stages" section, you'll find a "Refrigerator Sheet" that very briefly highlights the book's most important points. You can photocopy this sheet and place it on the refrigerator, so that you and everyone who loves your kids—parents, babysitters, grandparents, and so on—can work together on behalf of your children's overall well-being.

As we hope you'll see, we're keeping you in mind as we work to make this book as accessible and easy to read as possible. As scientists, we've emphasized precision and accuracy; as parents, we've aimed for practical understanding. And we've wrestled with this tension and carefully considered how best to provide you with the latest and most important information, while doing it in a way that's clear, helpful, and immediately practical. While the book is certainly scientifically based, you aren't going to feel like you're in science class or reading an academic paper. Yes, it's brain science, and we're absolutely committed to remaining true to what research and science demonstrate. But we'll share this information in a way that welcomes you in, rather than leaving you out in the cold. We've both spent our careers taking complicated but vital scientific knowledge about the brain and boiling it down so that parents can understand it and immediately apply it in their interactions with their kids on a daily basis. So don't be scared off by the brain stuff. We think you'll find it fascinating, and much of the basic information is actually pretty simple to understand, as well as easy to use. (If you *are* interested in more of the details of the science behind what we're presenting in these pages, take a look at Dan's books *Mindsight* and *The Developing Mind,* 2nd edition.)

Thanks for joining us on this journey toward a fuller knowledge of how you can truly help your kids be happier, healthier, and more fully themselves. With an understanding of the brain, you can be more intentional about what you teach your kids, how you respond to them, and why. You can then do much more than merely survive. By giving your children repeated experiences that develop the whole brain, you will face fewer everyday parenting crises. But more than that, understanding integration will let you know your child more deeply, respond more effectively to difficult situations, and intentionally build a foundation for a lifetime of love and happiness. As a result, not only will your child thrive, both now and into adulthood, but you and your whole family will as well.

Please visit us at our website and tell us about your whole-brain parenting experiences. We look forward to hearing from you.

Dan and Tina
www.WholeBrainChild.com

The
Whole-Brain
Child

CHAPTER 1

Parenting with the Brain in Mind

Parents are often experts about their children's bodies. They know that a temperature above 98.6 degrees is a fever. They know to clean out a cut so it doesn't get infected. They know which foods are most likely to leave their child wired before bedtime.

But even the most caring, best-educated parents often lack basic information about their child's brain. Isn't this surprising? Especially when you consider the central role the brain plays in virtually every aspect of a child's life that parents care about: discipline, decision making, self-awareness, school, relationships, and so on. In fact, the brain pretty much determines who we are and what we do. And since the brain itself is significantly shaped by the experiences we offer as parents, knowing about the way the brain changes in response to our parenting can help us to nurture a stronger, more resilient child.

So we want to introduce you to the whole-brain perspective. We'd like to explain some fundamental concepts about the brain and help you apply your new knowledge in ways that will make parenting easier and more meaningful. We're not saying that raising a whole-brain child will get rid of all the frustrations that come with parenting. *But by understanding a few simple and easy-to-master basics about how the brain works, you'll be able to better understand your child, respond more effectively to difficult situations, and build a foundation for social, emotional, and mental health.* What you do as a parent matters, and we'll provide you with straightforward, scientifically based ideas that will help you build a strong relationship with your child that can help shape his brain well and give him the best foundation for a healthy and happy life.

Let us tell you a story that illustrates how useful this information can be for parents.

Eea Woo Woo

One day Marianna received a call at work telling her that her two-year-old son, Marco, had been in a car accident with his babysitter. Marco was fine, but the babysitter, who was driving, had been taken to the hospital in an ambulance.

Marianna, a principal at an elementary school, frantically rushed to the scene of the accident, where she was told that the babysitter had experienced an epileptic seizure while driving. Marianna found a firefighter unsuccessfully attempting to console her toddler. She took Marco in her arms, and he immediately began to calm down as she comforted him.

As soon as he stopped crying, Marco began telling Marianna what had happened. Using his two-year-old language, which only his parents and babysitter would be able to understand, Marco continually repeated the phrase "Eea woo woo." "Eea" is his word for "Sophia," the name of his beloved babysitter, and "woo woo" refers to his version of the siren on a fire truck (or in this case, an ambulance). By repeatedly telling his mother "Eea woo woo," Marco was focusing on the detail of the story that mattered most to him: Sophia had been taken away from him.

In a situation like this, many of us would be tempted to assure Marco that Sophia would be fine, then immediately focus on something else to get the child's mind off the situation: "Let's go get some ice cream!" In the days that followed, many parents would try to avoid upsetting their child by not discussing the accident. The problem with the "let's go get some ice cream" approach is that it leaves the child confused about what happened and why. He is still full of big and scary emotions, but he isn't allowed (or helped) to deal with them in an effective way.

Marianna didn't make that mistake. She had taken Tina's classes on parenting and the brain, and she immediately put what she knew to good use. That night and over the next week, when Marco's mind continually brought him back to the car crash, Marianna helped him retell the story over and over again. She'd say, "Yes, you and Sophia were in an accident, weren't you?" At this point, Marco would stretch out his arms and shake them, imitating Sophia's seizure. Marianna would continue, "Yes, Sophia had a seizure and started shaking, and the car crashed, didn't it?" Marco's next statement was, of course, the familiar "Eea woo woo," to which Marianna would respond, "That's right. The woo woo came and took Sophia to the doctor. And now she's all better. Remember when we went to see her yesterday? She's doing just fine, isn't she?"

In allowing Marco to repeatedly retell the story, Marianna was helping him understand what had happened so he could begin to deal with it emotionally. Since she knew the importance of helping her son's brain process the frightening experience, she helped him tell and retell the events so that he could process his fear and go on with his daily routines in a healthy and balanced way. Over the next few days, Marco brought up the accident less and less, until it became just another of his life experiences—albeit an important one.

As you read the following pages, you'll learn specifics about why Marianna responded as she did, and why, both practically and neurologically, it was so helpful to her son. You'll be able to apply your new knowledge about the brain in numerous ways that make parenting your own child more manageable and meaningful.

The concept at the heart of Marianna's response, and of this book, is *integration*. A clear understanding of integration will give you the power to completely transform the way you think about parenting your kids. It can help you enjoy them more and better prepare them to live emotionally rich and rewarding lives.

WHAT IS INTEGRATION AND WHY DOES IT MATTER?

Most of us don't think about the fact that our brain has many different parts with different jobs. For example, you have a left side of the brain that helps you think logically and organize thoughts into sentences, and a right side that helps you experience emotions and read nonverbal cues. You also have a "reptile brain" that allows you to act instinctually and make split-second survival decisions, and a "mammal brain" that leads you toward connection and relationships. One part of your brain is devoted to dealing with memory; another to making moral and ethical decisions. It's almost as if your brain has multiple personalities—some rational, some irrational; some reflective, some reactive. No wonder we can seem like different people at different times!

The key to thriving is to help these parts work well together—to integrate them. Integration takes the distinct parts of your brain and helps them work together as a whole. It's similar to what happens in the body, which has different organs to perform different jobs: the lungs breathe air, the heart pumps blood, the stomach digests food. For the body to be healthy, these organs all need to be integrated. In other words, they each need to do their individual job while also working together as a whole. Integration is simply that: linking different elements together to make a well-functioning whole. Just as with the healthy functioning of the body, your brain can't perform at its best unless its different parts work together in a coordinated and balanced way. That's what integration does: it coordinates and balances the separate regions of the brain that it links together. It's easy to see when our kids aren't integrated—they become overwhelmed by their emotions, confused and chaotic. They can't respond calmly and capably to the situation at hand. Tantrums, meltdowns, aggression, and most of the other challenging experiences of parenting—and life—are a result of a loss of integration, also known as dis-integration.

We want to help our children become better integrated so they can use their whole brain in a coordinated way. For example, we want them to be *horizontally integrated,* so that their left-brain logic can work well with their right-brain emotion. We also want them to be *vertically integrated,* so that the physically higher parts of their brain, which let them thoughtfully consider their actions, work well with the lower parts, which are more concerned with instinct, gut reactions, and survival.

The way integration actually takes place is fascinating, and it's something that most people aren't aware of. In recent years, scientists have developed brain-scanning technology that allows researchers to study the brain in ways that were never before possible. This new technology has confirmed much of what we previously believed about the brain. However, one of the surprises that has shaken the very foundations of neuroscience is the discovery that the brain is actually "plastic," or moldable. This means that the brain physically changes throughout the course of our lives, not just in childhood, as we had previously assumed.

What molds our brain? Experience. Even into old age, our experiences actually change the physical structure of the brain. When we undergo an experience, our brain cells—called neurons—become active, or "fire." The brain has one hundred billion neurons, each with an average of ten thousand connections to other neurons. The ways in which particular circuits in the brain are activated determines the nature of our mental activity, ranging from perceiving sights or sounds to more abstract thought and reasoning. When neurons fire together, they grow new connections between them. Over time, the connections that result from firing lead to "rewiring" in the brain. This is incredibly exciting news. It means that we aren't held captive for the rest of our lives by the way our brain works at this moment—we can actually rewire it so that we can be healthier and happier. This is true not only for children and adolescents, but also for each of us across the life span.

Right now, your child's brain is constantly being wired and rewired, and the experiences you provide will go a long way toward determining the structure of her brain. No pressure, right? Don't worry, though. Nature has provided that the basic architecture of the brain will develop well given proper food, sleep, and stimulation. Genes, of course, play a large role in how people turn out, especially in terms of temperament. But findings from various areas in developmental psychology suggest that everything that happens to us—the music we hear, the people we love, the books we read, the kind of discipline we receive, the emotions we feel—profoundly affects the way our brain develops. In other words, on top of our basic brain architecture and our inborn temperament, parents have much they can do to provide the kinds of experiences that will help develop a resilient, well-integrated brain. This book will show you how to use everyday experiences to help your child's brain become more and more integrated.

For example, children whose parents talk with them about their experiences tend to have better access to the memories of those experiences. Parents who speak with their children about their feelings have children who develop emotional intelligence and can understand their own and other people's feelings more fully. Shy children whose parents nurture a sense of courage by offering supportive explorations of the world tend to lose their behavioral inhibition, while those who are excessively protected or insensitively thrust into anxiety-provoking experiences without support tend to maintain their shyness.

There is a whole field of the science of child development and attachment backing up this view—and the new findings in the field of neuroplasticity support the perspective that parents can directly shape the unfolding growth of their child's brain according to what experiences they offer. For example, hours of screen time—playing video games, watching television, texting—will wire the brain in certain ways. Educational activities, sports, and music will wire it in other ways. Spending time with family and friends and learning about relationships, especially with face-to-face interactions, will wire it in yet other ways. Everything that happens to us affects the way the brain develops.

This wire-and-rewire process is what integration is all about: giving our children experiences to create connections between different parts of the brain. When these parts collaborate, they create and reinforce the integrative fibers that link different parts of the brain. As a result, they are connected in more powerful ways and can work together even more harmoniously. Just as individual singers in a choir can weave their distinct voices into a harmony that would be impossible for any one person to create, an integrated brain is capable of doing much more than its individual parts could accomplish alone.

That's what we want to do for each of our kids: help their brain become more integrated so they can use their mental resources to full capacity. This is exactly what Marianna did for Marco. When she helped him retell the story over and over again ("Eea woo woo"), she defused the scary and traumatic emotions in his right brain so that they didn't rule him. She did so by bringing in factual details and logic from his left brain—which, at two years old, is just beginning to develop—so that he could deal with the accident in a way that made sense to him.

If his mother hadn't helped him tell and understand the story, Marco's fears would have been left unresolved and could have surfaced in other ways. He might have developed a phobia about riding in cars or being separated from his parents, or his right brain might have raged out of control in other ways, causing him to tantrum frequently. Instead, by telling the story with Marco, Marianna helped focus his attention both on the actual details of the accident and on his emotions, which allowed him to use both the left and right sides of his brain together, literally strengthening their connection. (We'll explain this particular concept much more fully in chapter 2.) By helping him become better integrated, he could return to being a normal, developing two-year-old rather than dwelling on the fear and distress he had experienced.

Let's look at another example. Now that you and your siblings are adults, do you still fight over who gets to push the button for the elevator? Of course not. (Well, we hope not.) But do your kids squabble and bicker over this kind of issue? If they're typical kids, they do.

The reason behind this difference brings us back to the brain and integration. Sibling rivalry is like so many other issues that make parenting difficult—tantrums, disobedience, homework battles, discipline matters, and so on. As we'll explain in the coming chapters, these everyday parenting challenges result from a *lack of integration* within your child's brain. The reason her brain isn't always capable of integration is simple: it hasn't had time to develop. In fact, it's got a long way to go, since a person's brain isn't considered fully developed until she reaches her mid-twenties.

So that's the bad news: you have to wait for your child's brain to develop. That's right. No matter how brilliant you think your preschooler is, she does not have the brain of a ten-year-old, and won't for several years. The rate of brain maturation is largely influenced by the genes we inherit. But the degree of integration may be exactly what we can influence in our day-to-day parenting.

The good news is that by using everyday moments, you can influence how well your child's brain grows toward integration. First, you can develop the diverse elements of your child's brain by offering opportunities to exercise them. Second, you can facilitate integration so that the separate parts become better connected and work together in powerful ways. This isn't making your children grow up more quickly—it's simply helping them develop the many parts of themselves and integrate them. We're also not talking about wearing yourself (and your kids) out by frantically trying to fill every experience with significance and meaning. We're talking about simply being present with your children so you can help them become better integrated. As a result, they will thrive emotionally, intellectually, and socially. An integrated brain results in improved decision making, better control of body and emotions, fuller self-understanding, stronger relationships, and success in school. And it all begins with the experiences parents and other caregivers provide, which lay the groundwork for integration and mental health.

GET IN THE FLOW: NAVIGATING THE WATERS BETWEEN CHAOS AND RIGIDITY

Let's get a little more specific about what it looks like when a person—child or adult—is living in a state of integration. When a person is well integrated, he enjoys mental health and well-being. But that's not exactly easy to define. In fact, even though entire libraries have been written discussing mental *illness,* mental *health* is rarely defined. Dan has pioneered a definition of mental health that researchers and therapists around the world are now beginning to use. It's based on the concept of integration and involves an understanding of the complex dynamics surrounding relationships and the brain. A simple way to express it, though, is to describe mental health as our ability to remain in a "river of well-being."

Imagine a peaceful river running through the countryside. That's your river of well-being. Whenever you're in the water, peacefully floating along in your canoe, you feel like you're generally in a good relationship with the world around you. You have a clear understanding of yourself, other people, and your life. You can be flexible and adjust when situations change. You're stable and at peace.

Sometimes, though, as you float along, you veer too close to one of the river's two banks. This causes different problems, depending on which bank you approach. One bank represents chaos, where you feel out of control. Instead of floating in the peaceful river, you are caught up in the pull of tumultuous rapids, and confusion and turmoil rule the day. You need to move away from the bank of chaos and get back into the gentle flow of the river.

But don't go too far, because the other bank presents its own dangers. It's the bank of rigidity, which is the opposite of chaos. As opposed to being out of control, rigidity is when you are *imposing* control on everything and everyone around you. You become completely unwilling to adapt, compromise, or negotiate. Near the bank of rigidity, the water smells stagnant, and reeds and tree branches prevent your canoe from flowing in the river of well-being.

So one extreme is chaos, where there's a total lack of control. The other extreme is rigidity, where there's too much control, leading to a lack of flexibility and adaptability. We all move back and forth between these two banks as we go through our days—especially as we're trying to survive parenting. When we're closest to the banks of chaos or rigidity, we're farthest from mental and emotional health. The longer we can avoid either bank, the more time we spend enjoying the river of well-being. Much of our lives

as adults can be seen as moving along these paths—sometimes in the harmony of the flow of well-being, but sometimes in chaos, in rigidity, or zigzagging back and forth between the two. Harmony emerges from integration. Chaos and rigidity arise when integration is blocked.

All of this applies to our kids as well. They have their own little canoes, and they float down their own river of well-being. Many of the challenges we face as parents result from the times when our kids aren't in the flow, when they're either too chaotic or too rigid. Your three-year-old won't share his toy boat at the park? Rigidity. He erupts into crying, yelling, and throwing sand when his new friend takes the boat away? Chaos. What you can do is help guide your child back into the flow of the river, into a harmonious state that avoids both chaos and rigidity.

The same goes for older children. Your normally easygoing fifth-grader is crying hysterically because she didn't get the solo she wanted in the school play. She refuses to calm down and repeatedly tells you that she has the best voice in her grade. She's actually zigzagging back and forth between the banks of chaos and rigidity, as her emotions have clearly taken control of her logic. As a result, she stubbornly refuses to acknowledge that someone else might be just as talented. You can guide her back into the flow of well-being so that she can achieve better balance within herself and move into a more integrated state. (Don't worry—we'll offer you plenty of ways to do this.)

Virtually all survival moments fit into this framework in one way or another. We think you may be astounded to see how well the ideas of chaos and rigidity help you understand your child's most difficult behaviors. These concepts actually allow you to "take the temperature" of how well integrated your child is at any given moment. If you see chaos and/or rigidity, you know she's not in a state of integration. Likewise, when she *is* in a state of integration, she demonstrates the qualities we associate with someone who is mentally and emotionally healthy: she is flexible, adaptive, stable, and able to understand herself and the world around her. The powerful and practical approach of integration enables us to see the many ways in which our children—or we ourselves—experience chaos and rigidity because integration has been blocked. When we become aware of this idea, we can then create and carry out strategies that promote integration in our kids' lives and in our own. These are the day-to-day whole-brain strategies we'll explore in each of the following chapters.

Two Brains Are Better Than One

Integrating the Left and the Right

Thomas's four-year-old daughter, Katie, loved her preschool and never minded saying goodbye to her dad when it was time for him to leave—until the day she got sick in class. Her teacher phoned Thomas, who came to pick her up right away. The next day, Katie began crying when it was time to get ready for school, even though by then she was feeling fine. The same thing happened morning after morning for the next few days. He could eventually get her dressed, but things only got worse when they arrived at school.

As Thomas put it, Katie would increasingly "freak out" once they got out of their car in the school parking lot. First she'd begin to practice some sort of civil disobedience as they approached the school building. She would walk alongside her father, but as she somehow made her tiny body heavier than a grand piano, her resistance would turn their stroll into more of a drag. Then, when they reached the classroom, she would squeeze her dad's hand harder and harder and perform the classic "power lean," putting all of her baby-grand weight on Thomas's leg. When he could finally extricate himself from her clutches and exit the room, he would hear her shout above all the noise of the other kids, "I'll die if you leave me!"

This type of separation anxiety is very normal for young children. School can be a scary place at times. But as Thomas explained, "Katie absolutely lived for school before she got sick. She loved the activities, the friends, the stories. And she adored her teacher."

So what happened? How did the simple experience of getting sick create such an extreme and irrational fear in Katie, and what was the best way for Thomas to respond? His immediate goal: come up with a strategy to get Katie to willingly attend school again. That was his "survive" goal. But he also wanted to turn this difficult experience into an opportunity that would benefit Katie in both the short and the long term. That was his "thrive" goal.

We'll come back to how Thomas handled the situation, using his basic knowledge about the brain to turn a survival moment into an opportunity to help his daughter thrive. Specifically, he understood what we're going to show you now: some simple principles about how the two different sides of the brain work.

LEFT BRAIN, RIGHT BRAIN: AN INTRODUCTION

You probably know that your brain is divided into two hemispheres. Not only are these two sides of the brain anatomically separate; they also function very differently. Some people even say that the two hemispheres have their own distinct personalities, each side with a "mind of its own." The scientific community refers to the way the different sides of the brain influence us as left-hemisphere and right-hemisphere modalities. But for simplicity's sake, we'll just go with the common usage and talk about your left brain and your right brain.

Your left brain loves and desires order. It is *logical, literal, linguistic* (it likes words), and *linear* (it puts things in a sequence or order). The left brain *loves* that all four of these words begin with the letter *L*. (It also loves lists.)

The right brain, on the other hand, is holistic and nonverbal, sending and receiving signals that allow us to communicate, such as facial expressions, eye contact, tone of voice, posture, and gestures. Instead of details and order, our right brain cares about the big picture—the meaning and feel of an experience—and specializes in images, emotions, and personal memories. We get a "gut feeling" or "heart-felt sense" from our right brain. Some say the right brain is more intuitive and emotional, and we'll use those terms in the following pages as a helpful shorthand to talk about what the right brain does. But keep in mind that technically, it's more accurate to talk about this side of the brain as more directly influenced by the body and lower brain areas, which allow it to receive and interpret emotional information. It can get complicated, but the basic idea is that while the left brain is logical, linguistic, and literal, the right brain is emotional, nonverbal, experiential, and autobiographical—and it doesn't care at all that these words don't begin with the same letter.

You might think of it this way: the left brain cares about the *letter of the law* (more of those *L*'s). As you know, as kids get older they get really good at using this left-brain thinking: "I didn't shove her! I pushed her." The right brain, on the other hand, cares about the *spirit of the law,* the emotions and experiences of relationships. The left focuses on the text—the right is about the context. It was the nonlogical, emotional right brain that prompted Katie to yell to her father, "I'll die if you leave me!"

In terms of development, very young children are right-hemisphere dominant, especially during their first three years. They haven't mastered the ability to use logic and words to express their feelings, and they live their lives completely in the moment—which is why they will drop everything to squat down and fully absorb themselves in watching a ladybug crawl along the sidewalk, not caring one bit that they are late for their toddler music class. Logic, responsibilities, and time don't exist for them yet. But when a toddler begins asking "Why?" all the time, you know that the left brain is beginning to really kick in. Why? Because our left brain likes to know the linear cause-effect relationships in the world—and to express that logic with language.

Two Halves Make a Whole: Combining the Left and the Right

In order to live balanced, meaningful, and creative lives full of connected relationships, it's crucial that our two hemispheres work together. The very architecture of the brain is designed this way. For example, the corpus callosum is a bundle of fibers that runs along the center of the brain, connecting the right hemisphere with the left. The communication that takes place between the two sides of our brain is conducted across these fibers, allowing the two hemispheres to work as a team—which is exactly what we want for our kids. We want them to become *horizontally integrated,* so that the two sides of their brain can act in harmony. That way, our children will value both their logic *and* their emotions; they will be well balanced and able to understand themselves and the world at large.

The brain has two sides for a reason: with each side having specialized functions, we can achieve more complex goals and carry out more intricate, sophisticated tasks. Significant problems arise when the two sides of our brain are *not* integrated and we end up coming at our experiences primarily from one side or the other. Using only the right or left brain would be like trying to swim using only one arm. We might be able to do it, but wouldn't we be a lot more successful—and avoid going in circles—if we used both arms together?

It's the same with the brain. Think about our emotions, for example. They're absolutely crucial if we are to live meaningfully, but we don't want them to completely rule our lives. If our right brain took over and we ignored the logic of our left brain, we would feel like we were drowning in images, bodily sensations, and what could feel like an emotional flood. But at the same time, we don't want to use only our left brain, divorcing our logic and language from our feelings and personal experiences. That would feel like living in an emotional desert.

The goal is to avoid living in an emotional flood *or* an emotional desert. We want to allow our nonrational images, autobiographical memories, and vital emotions to play their important roles, but we also want to integrate them with the parts of ourselves that give our lives order and structure. When Katie freaked out about being left at preschool, she was working mostly from her right brain. As a result, Thomas witnessed an illogical emotional flood, where Katie's emotional right brain wasn't working in a co-ordinated way with her logical left brain.

Here it's important to note that it's not only our children's emotional floods that cause problems. An emotional desert, where feelings and the right brain are ignored or denied, is no healthier than a flood. We see this response more often in older children. For example, Dan tells a story of an exchange with a twelve-year-old girl who came to see him with a scenario many of us have experienced:

> Amanda mentioned a fight she'd had with her best friend. I knew from her mother that this argument had been extremely painful for Amanda, but as she talked about it, she just shrugged and stared out the window, saying, "I don't really care if we never talk again. She annoys me anyway." The expression on her face seemed cold and resigned, but in the subtle quiver of her lower lips and the gentle opening and closing of her eyelids, almost like a tremor, I could sense the right-hemisphere nonverbal signals revealing what we might call her "real feelings." Rejection is painful, and at this moment, Amanda's way of dealing with that sense of vulnerability was to "retreat to the left," running to the arid (but predictable and controllable) emotional desert of the left side of her brain.
>
> I had to help her understand that even though it was painful to think about the conflict with her friend, she needed to pay attention to, and even honor, what was going on in her right brain, since the right brain is more directly connected to our bodily sensations and the input from lower parts of the brain that combine together to create our emotions. In this way, all of the imagery, sensations, and autobiographical memories from the right are infused with emotion. When we're upset, it can feel safer to withdraw from this unpredictable right-sided awareness and retreat into the more predictable and controlled logical land of the left.
>
> The key to helping Amanda was for me to attune to those real feelings gently. I didn't point out abruptly that she was hid-

ing, even from herself, how this important person in her life had hurt her. Instead, I allowed myself to feel what she was feeling, then tried to communicate from my right brain to her right brain. Using my facial expressions and posture, I let her know that I was really tuning in to her emotions. That attunement helped her "feel felt"—to know that she was not alone, that I was interested in what she was feeling inside, not only what she was doing on the outside. Then, once we had established this sense of connection between us, words came more naturally for both of us, and we could begin to get to the bottom of what was going on inside of her. By asking her to tell the story about the fight with her best friend and having her pause the story at different times to observe subtle shifts in her feelings, I was able to reintroduce Amanda to her real emotions and to help her deal with them in a productive way. This is how I tried to connect with both her right brain with its feelings, bodily sensations, and images and with her left brain, with its words and ability to tell the linear story of her experience. When we see how this happens in the brain, we can understand how linking the two sides to each other can completely change the outcome of an interaction.

We don't want our children to hurt. But we also want them to do more than simply get through their difficult times; we want them to face their troubles and grow from them. When Amanda retreated to the left, hiding from all of the painful emotions that were running through her right brain, she denied an important part of herself that she needed to acknowledge.

Denial of our emotions isn't the only danger we face when we rely too heavily on our left brain. We can also become too literal, leaving us without a sense of perspective, where we miss the meaning that comes from putting things in context (a specialty of the right brain). This is part of what causes your eight-year-old to become defensive and angry sometimes when you innocently joke around with her. Remember that the right brain is in charge of reading nonverbal cues. So especially if she is tired or moody, she might focus only on your words and miss your playful tone of voice and the wink that went with it.

Tina recently witnessed a funny example of what can happen when the literal left brain takes over too much. When her youngest son turned one, she ordered his cake from a local grocery store. She requested a "cupcake cake," which is a group of cupcakes frosted to look like one big cake. When she placed the order, she asked the decorator to write her son's name—J.P.— on the cupcakes. Unfortunately, when she picked up the cake before the party, she immediately noticed a problem that demonstrates what can happen when a person becomes too left-brain literal.

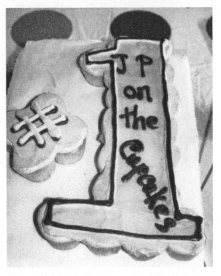

When Tina told the baker she wanted the cake to say J.P. on the cupcakes, a literal, left-brain interpretation was not what she expected.

The goal, then, is to help our kids learn to use both sides of the brain together—to integrate the left and right hemispheres. Remember the river of well-being discussed earlier, with chaos as one bank and rigidity as the other. We defined mental health as remaining in the harmonious flow between these two extremes. By helping our kids connect left and right, we give them a better chance of avoiding the banks of chaos and rigidity, and of living in the flexible current of mental health and happiness.

Integrating the left brain with the right helps to keep children from floating too close to one bank or the other. When the raw emotions in their right brain are not combined with the logic of the left, they will be like Katie, floating too close to the bank of chaos. That means we need to help them bring in the left brain to get some perspective and handle their emotions in a positive way. Likewise, if they're denying their emotions and retreating to the left, as Amanda was doing, they're hugging the bank of rigidity. In that case, we need to help them bring in more of the right brain so they can be open to new input and experiences.

So how do we promote horizontal integration in our child's brain? Here are two strategies you can use right away when "integration opportunities" arise in your family. By using these techniques, you'll be taking immediate steps toward integrating the left and right hemispheres of your child's brain.

What You Can Do:
Helping Your Child Work from Both Sides of the Brain

Whole-Brain Strategy #1:
Connect and Redirect: Surfing Emotional Waves

One night Tina's seven-year-old son reappeared in the living room shortly after going to bed, explaining that he couldn't sleep. He was clearly upset and explained, "I'm mad that you never leave me a note in the middle of the night!" Surprised at this unusual outburst, Tina replied, "I didn't know you wanted me to." His response was to unleash a whole litany of rapid-fire complaints: "You never do anything nice for me, and I'm mad because my birthday isn't for ten more months, and I hate homework!"

Logical? No. Familiar? Yes. All parents experience times when their children say things and get upset about issues that don't seem to make sense. An encounter like this can be frustrating, especially when you expect your child to be old enough to act rationally and hold a logical conversation. All of a sudden, though, he becomes upset about something ridiculous, and it seems that absolutely no amount of reasoning on your part will help.

Based on our knowledge of the two sides of the brain, we know that Tina's son was experiencing big waves of right-brain emotions without much left-brain logical balance. At a moment like this, one of the least effective things Tina could do would be to jump right in and defend herself ("*Of course* I do nice things for you!") or to argue with her son about his faulty logic ("There's nothing I can do about making your birthday come sooner. As for the homework, that's just something that you've got to do"). This type of left-brain, logical response would hit an unreceptive right-brain brick wall and create a gulf between them. After all, his logical left brain was nowhere to be found at that moment. So, had

Tina responded with her left, her son would have felt like she didn't understand him or care about his feelings. He was in a right-brain, nonrational, emotional flood, and a left-brain response would have been a lose-lose approach.

Even though it was practically automatic (and very tempting) to ask him "What are you talking about?" or to tell him to go back to bed immediately, Tina stopped herself. Instead she used the connect-and-redirect technique. She pulled him close, rubbed his back, and with a nurturing tone of voice, said, "Sometimes it's just really hard, isn't it? I would never forget about you. You are always in my mind, and I always want you to know how special you are to me." She held him while he explained that he sometimes feels that his younger brother gets more of her attention, and that homework takes too much of his free time. As he spoke, she could feel him relax and soften. He felt heard and cared for. Then she briefly addressed the specific issues he had brought up, since he was now more receptive to problem solving and planning, and they agreed to talk more in the morning.

In a moment like this, parents wonder whether their child is really in need or just trying to stall bedtime. Whole-brain parenting doesn't mean letting yourself be manipulated or reinforcing bad behavior. On the contrary, by understanding how your child's brain works, you can create cooperation much more quickly and often with far less drama. In this case, because Tina understood what was happening in her son's brain, she saw that the most effective response was to connect with his right brain. She listened to him and comforted him, using her own right brain, and in less than five minutes he was back in bed. If, on the other hand, she had played the heavy and come down hard on him for getting out of bed, using left-brain logic and the letter of the law, they would have both become increasingly upset—and it would have been a lot more than five minutes before he calmed down enough to sleep.

More important, Tina's was a more caring and nurturing response. Even though her son's issues seemed silly and perhaps illogical to her, he genuinely felt that things weren't fair and that he had legitimate complaints. By connecting with him, right brain to right brain, she was able to communicate that she was tuned in to how he was feeling. Even if he was stalling, this right-brain response was the most effective approach, since it let her not only meet his need for connection, but also redirect him to bed more quickly. Instead of fighting against the huge waves of his emotional flood, Tina surfed them by responding to his right brain.

This story points out an important insight: *when a child is upset, logic often won't work until we have responded to the right brain's emotional needs.* We call this emotional connection "attunement," which is how we connect deeply with another person and allow them to "feel felt." When parent and child are tuned in to each other, they experience a sense of joining together.

Tina's approach with her son is one that we call the "connect and redirect" method, and it begins with helping our kids "feel felt" before we try to solve problems or address the situation logically. Here's how it works:

Step 1: Connect with the Right

In our society, we're trained to work things out using our words and our logic. But when your four-year-old is absolutely furious because he can't walk on the ceiling like Spider-Man (as Tina's son once was), that's probably not the best time to give him an introductory lesson in the laws of physics. Or when your eleven-year-old is feeling hurt because it seems that his sister is receiving preferential treatment (as Dan's son felt on occasion), the appropriate response isn't to get out a scorecard showing that you reprimand each of your children in equal measure.

Instead, we can use these opportunities to realize that at these moments, logic isn't our primary vehicle for bringing some sort of sanity to the conversation. (Seems counterintuitive, doesn't it?) It's also crucial to keep in mind that no matter how nonsensical and frustrating our child's feelings may seem to us, they are real and important to our child. It's vital that we treat them as such in our response.

During Tina's conversation with her son, she appealed to his right brain by acknowledging his feelings. She also used nonverbal signals like physical touch, empathetic facial expressions, a nurturing tone of voice, and nonjudgmental listening. In other words, she used her right brain to connect and communicate with his right brain. This right-to-right attunement helped bring his brain into balance, or into a more integrated state. *Then* she could begin to appeal to her son's left brain and address the specific issues he had raised. In other words, then it was time for step 2, which helps to integrate the left and the right.

Step 2: Redirect with the Left

After responding with the right, Tina could then redirect with the left. She could redirect him by logically explaining how hard she works to be fair, by promising to leave a note while he slept, and by strategizing with him about his next birthday and about how to make homework more fun. (They did some of this that night, but most of it came the following day.)

Once she had connected with him right brain to right brain, it was much easier to connect left to left and deal with the issues in a rational manner. By first *connecting* with his right brain, she could then *redirect* with the left brain through logical explanation and planning, which required that his left hemisphere join the conversation. This approach allowed him to use both sides of his brain in an integrated, coordinated way.

We're not saying that "connect and redirect" will always do the trick. After all, there are times when a child is simply past the point of no return and the emotional waves just need to crash until the storm passes. Or the child may simply need to eat or get some sleep. Like Tina, you might decide to wait until your child is in a more integrated state of mind to talk logically with her about his feelings and behaviors.

We're also not recommending permissiveness or letting your boundaries slide simply because a child isn't thinking logically. Rules about respect and behavior aren't thrown out the window simply because a child's left hemisphere is disengaged. For example, whatever behavior is inappropriate in your family—being disrespectful, hurting someone, throwing things—should remain off-limits even in moments of high emotion. You may need to stop destructive behavior and remove your child from the situation before you begin to connect and redirect. But with the whole-

INSTEAD OF COMMAND AND DEMAND...

...TRY CONNECT AND REDIRECT

brain approach, we understand that it's generally a good idea to discuss misbehavior and its consequences *after* the child has calmed down, since moments of emotional flooding are not the best times for lessons to be learned. A child can be much more receptive once the left brain is working again, and discipline can therefore be much more effective. It's as if you are a lifeguard who swims out, puts your arms around your child, and helps him to shore *before* telling him not to swim out so far next time.

The key here is that when your child is drowning in a right-brain emotional flood, you'll do yourself (and your child) a big favor if you connect before you redirect. This approach can be a life preserver that helps keep your child's head above water, and keeps you from being pulled under along with him.

Whole-Brain Strategy #2:
Name It to Tame It: Telling Stories to Calm Big Emotions

A toddler falls and scrapes an elbow. A kindergartner loses a beloved pet. A fifth-grader faces a bully at school. When a child experiences painful, disappointing, or scary moments, it can be overwhelming, with big emotions and bodily sensations flooding the right brain. When this happens, we as parents can help bring the left hemisphere into the picture so that the child can begin to understand what's happening. One of the best ways to promote this type of integration is to help retell the story of the frightening or painful experience.

Bella, for instance, was nine years old when the toilet over-flowed when she flushed, and the experience of watching the water rise and pour onto the floor left her unwilling (and practically unable) to flush the toilet afterward. When Bella's father, Doug, learned about the "name it to tame it" technique, he sat down with his daughter and retold the story of the time the toilet overflowed. He allowed her to tell as much of the story as she could and helped to fill in the details, including the lingering fear she had felt about flushing since that experience. After retelling the story several times, Bella's fears lessened and eventually went away.

Why was retelling the story so effective? Essentially, what Doug did was to help his daughter bring her left brain and her right brain together so she could make sense of what had happened. When she talked through the moment the water had started spilling on the floor and how she'd felt worried and afraid, her two hemispheres were working together in an integrated way. She engaged her left brain by putting the details in order and the experience into words, and then brought in her right brain by revisiting the emotions she felt. In this way, Doug helped his daughter *name* her fears and emotions so that she could then *tame* them.

There may be times when our kids won't want to tell the story when we ask them to. We need to respect their desires about how and when to talk—especially because pressuring them to share will only backfire. (Think about the times you prefer solitude and don't feel like talking—does prodding ever entice you to talk and share your inner feelings?) Instead, we can gently encourage them by beginning the story and asking them to fill in the details, and if they're not interested, we can give them space and talk later.

Your child is more likely to be responsive if you are strategic about when you initiate this type of conversation. Make sure you are both in a good frame of mind. Seasoned parents and child therapists will also tell you that some of the best conversations with children take place while something else is happening. Children are much more apt to share and talk while building something, playing cards, or riding in the car than when you sit down and look them right in the face and ask them to open up. Another approach you can take if your child doesn't feel like talking is to ask her to draw a picture of the event or, if she's old enough, write about it. If you sense that she is reluctant to talk to you, encourage her to talk to someone else—a friend, another adult, or even a sibling who will be a good listener.

Parents know how powerful storytelling can be when it comes to distracting their kids or calming them down, but most people don't realize the science behind this powerful force. The right side of our brain processes our emotions and autobiographical memories, but our left side is what makes sense of these feelings and recollections. Healing from a difficult experience emerges when the left side works with the right to tell our life stories. When children learn to pay attention to and share their own stories, they can respond in healthy ways to everything from a scraped elbow to a major loss or trauma.

What kids often need, especially when they experience strong emotions, is to have someone help them use their left brain to make sense of what's going on—to put things in order and to name these big and scary right-brain feelings so they can deal with them effectively. This is what storytelling does: it allows us to understand ourselves and our world by using both our left and right hemispheres together. To tell a story that makes sense, the left brain must put things in order, using words and logic. The right brain contributes the bodily sensations, raw emotions, and personal memories, so we can see the whole picture and communicate our experience. This is the scientific explanation behind why journaling and talking about a difficult event can be so powerful in helping us heal. In fact, research shows that merely assigning a name or label to what we feel literally calms down the activity of the emotional circuitry in the right hemisphere.

For this same reason, it's important for kids of all ages to tell their stories, as it helps them try to understand their emotions and the events that occur in their lives. Sometimes parents avoid talking about upsetting experiences, thinking that doing so will reinforce their children's pain or make things worse. Actually, telling the story is often exactly what children need, both to make sense of the event and to move on to a place where they can feel better about what happened. (Remember Marianna's son, Marco, from the "Eea woo woo" story in chapter 1?) The drive to understand why things happen to us is so strong that the brain will continue to try making sense of an experience until it succeeds. As parents, we can help this process along through storytelling.

That's what Thomas did with Katie, the preschooler who was screaming about dying if her father left her at school. Even though he felt frustrated with the situation, he resisted the urge to dismiss and deny Katie's experiences. Because of what he had learned, he recognized that his daughter's brain was linking several events together: being dropped off at school, getting sick, having her father leave, and feeling afraid. As a result, when it came time to pack up and go to school, her brain and body started telling her, "Bad idea:

school = feeling sick = Dad gone = afraid." From that perspective, it made sense that she didn't want to go to school.

Realizing this, Thomas used his knowledge about the brain's two hemispheres. He knew that small children like Katie are typically right-hemisphere dominant and haven't mastered their ability to use logic and words to express feelings. Katie felt the strong emotions, but she wasn't able to understand and communicate them clearly. As a result, they had become overpowering. He also knew that autobiographical memory is stored in the right side of the brain, and understood that the details of her getting sick had become linked in her memory and caused her right hemisphere to shift into overdrive.

Once Thomas grasped all of this, he knew he needed to help Katie make sense of those emotions by using her left hemisphere—by bringing in logic, putting the events in order, and assigning words to her feelings. The way he did this was by helping her tell a story about what had happened that day so that she could use both sides of her brain together. He told her, "I know you've been having a hard time going to school since you got sick. Let's try to remember the day you felt sick at school. First, we got ready for school, didn't we? Remember, you wanted to wear your red pants, we had waffles with blueberries, and then you brushed your teeth? We got to school and we hugged and said goodbye. You started to paint at the activity table and I waved bye to you. And then what happened after I left?"

Katie responded that she got sick. Thomas continued, "Right. And I know that didn't feel good, did it? But then Ms. LaRussa took really good care of you and knew you needed Daddy, so she called me and I came right away. Aren't you lucky to have a teacher that took care of you until Daddy could come? And then what happened? I took care of you and you felt better." Thomas then emphasized that he came right away and that everything was OK, and he assured Katie that he would always be there anytime she needed him.

By putting these narrative details in order like this, Thomas allowed his daughter to begin to make sense of what she was experiencing with her emotions and in her body. He then began to help her create some new associations that school is safe and fun, reminding her of various aspects of her school that she loved. They wrote and illustrated a book together that told the story and featured her favorite places in her classroom. As kids often will, Katie wanted to read her homemade book over and over.

Before long, she regained her love of school, and the experience didn't have such power over her anymore. In fact, she learned that she could overcome fear with the support of the people who love her. As Katie grows, her father will continue to help her make sense of her experiences; this storytelling process will become a natural way for her to deal with difficult situations, giving her a powerful tool for dealing with adversity into adulthood and throughout her life.

Even children much younger than Katie—as young as ten to twelve months—respond well to telling stories. For example, imagine a toddler who's fallen down and skinned her knee. Her right brain, which is completely in the present moment and in touch with her body and fear, feels pain. On some level, she worries that the pain may never go away. When the mother retells the story of the fall, putting words and order to the experience, she helps her daughter engage and develop her left brain, explaining what happened—she simply fell down—so that she can understand why she's hurting.

Don't underestimate the power of a story to hold a child's attention. Try this if you have a little one—you'll be amazed at how helpful it can be, and how eager he'll be to help tell future stories when he's been hurt or feels afraid.

This "name it to tame it" technique is just as powerful with older kids. One mother we know, Laura, used it with her son, Jack, who had been in a minor (but still scary) biking accident when he was ten and felt nervous anytime he thought about going out on a bicycle. Here's how she helped him tell the story so that he could begin to understand what was going on inside.

LAURA: Do you remember what happened when you fell?
JACK: I was looking at you when we were crossing the street. And I didn't see the grate of the sewer.

INSTEAD OF DISMISS AND DENY...

...TRY NAME IT TO TAME IT

LAURA: And what happened next?

JACK: My wheel got caught and the bike fell over on me.

LAURA: And that was frightening, wasn't it?

JACK: Yeah, I didn't know what to do . . . I just went down in the street, and I couldn't even see what was happening.

LAURA: That must have been scary, to have something happen out of nowhere. Do you remember what happened next?

Laura went on to help Jack recount the whole experience. Together they discussed how, in the end, the ordeal was resolved by some tears, comforting, Band-Aids, and bike repairs. Then they talked about watching out for sewer grates and being aware of oncoming traffic, which helped Jack free himself from some of the feelings of helplessness.

The details of a conversation like this will obviously change along with the situation. But notice how Laura drew the story out of her son, letting him take an active role in the storytelling process. She acted primarily as a facilitator, helping get the facts of the event straight. This is how stories empower us to move forward and master the moments when we feel out of control. When we can give words to our frightening and painful experiences—when we literally *come to terms* with them—they often become much less frightening and painful. When we help our children name their pain and their fears, we help them tame them.

Whole-Brain Kids:
Teach Your Kids About the Two Sides of the Brain

In this chapter, we gave you several examples of how to help your kids integrate their left and right brain. It can also be helpful to talk to your children, and explain to them some basics about the information we've just covered. To help you along, here's something you can read with your kids. We've written it with five-to-nine-year-olds in mind, but you should make it your own and adapt it to fit the age and developmental stage of each child.

YOUR LEFT BRAIN AND YOUR RIGHT BRAIN

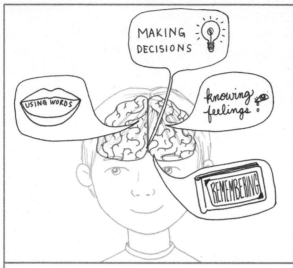

DO YOU KNOW THAT YOU HAVE MANY PARTS TO YOUR BRAIN AND THEY ALL DO DIFFERENT THINGS? IT'S ALMOST LIKE YOU HAVE DIFFERENT BRAINS WITH MINDS OF THEIR OWN. BUT WE CAN HELP THEM ALL GET ALONG AND HELP ONE ANOTHER.

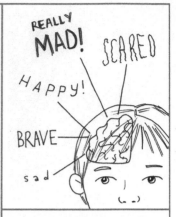

OUR RIGHT BRAIN LISTENS TO OUR BODY AND OTHER PARTS OF OUR BRAIN AND KNOWS ABOUT OUR BIG FEELINGS LIKE WHEN WE'RE HAPPY, OR BRAVE, OR SCARED, OR SAD, OR REALLY MAD. IT'S IMPORTANT THAT WE PAY ATTENTION TO THESE FEELINGS AND TALK ABOUT THEM.

SOMETIMES WHEN WE'RE UPSET AND WE DON'T TALK ABOUT IT, OUR FEELINGS CAN BUILD AND BUILD INSIDE US, LIKE A HUGE WAVE THAT WASHES OVER US AND MAKES US SAY OR DO THINGS WE DON'T MEAN.

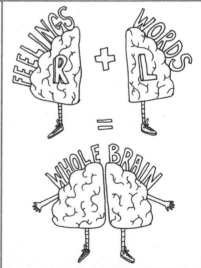

BUT THE LEFT BRAIN CAN HELP PUT OUR FEELINGS INTO WORDS. THEN OUR WHOLE BRAIN CAN WORK TOGETHER AS A TEAM AND WE CAN CALM DOWN.

FOR EXAMPLE:

ANNIE GOT SICK AND HAD TO MISS HER FRIEND'S BIRTHDAY PARTY. SHE WAS SO MAD ABOUT STAYING HOME THAT A HUGE ANGER WAVE GREW AND GREW AND WAS ABOUT TO CRASH DOWN ON HER.

ANNIE'S DAD HELPED HER TALK ABOUT WHAT SHE WAS FEELING.

WHEN SHE USED HER WORDS TO SAY HOW SHE FELT, HER LEFT BRAIN HELPED HER SURF THE BIG ANGER WAVE FROM HER RIGHT BRAIN, AND SHE RODE IT TO SHORE, CALM AND HAPPY.

Integrating Ourselves: Connecting Our Left and Right Brain

Now that you know more about the left and right sides of the brain, think about your own integration. When it comes to parenting, are you too right-brain dominant? Do you frequently get swept up in emotional floods, leaving your children drenched with your own chaos and fear? Or maybe your tendency is to live in a left-brain emotional desert, so you are rigid in your reactions and have a hard time reading and responding to your children's emotions and needs?

Here are the words of a mom we know who realized that she was primarily interacting with her young son using only one side of her own brain:

I was brought up in a military family. Needless to say, I am not very touchy-feely! I'm a veterinarian and a trained problem solver, which doesn't help me in the empathy department.

When my son would cry or become upset, I would try to get him to settle down so I could help him solve the problem. This was not helpful and sometimes exacerbated the crying, so I would walk away and wait until he calmed down.

Recently, I learned about trying to connect emotionally first—right brain to right brain, which was totally foreign to me. Now I hold my son, listen, and even try and help him tell his story, using both the left and right brain together. Then we talk about the behavior or solve the problem. Now I try to remember to connect first and solve second.

It took some practice, but when I related to my son emotionally first, using my right brain, along with my left, instead of using only my left, everything else went more smoothly and our relationship in general improved as well.

This mother realized that by ignoring parts of her own right brain, she was missing out on important opportunities to connect with her son and to enhance the development of his right brain.

One of the best ways to promote integration in our children is to become better integrated ourselves. (We'll discuss this more fully in chapter 6 when we explain mirror neurons.) When right and left brain are integrated, we can approach parenting from both a grounded, left-brained, rational place—one that lets us make important decisions, solve problems, and enforce boundaries—*and* from a right-brained, emotionally connected place where we're aware of the feelings and sensations of our body and emotions, so we can lovingly respond to our children's needs. Then we'll be parenting with *our* whole brain.

CHAPTER 3

Building the Staircase of the Mind

Integrating the Upstairs and Downstairs Brain

One afternoon Jill heard yelling and commotion in the bedroom of her six-year-old, Grant. Four-year-old Gracie had found her brother's treasure box and taken his "most rarest crystal," which she then lost. Jill arrived just in time to hear Gracie say, in her most spiteful voice, "It's just a dumb rock and I'm *glad* I lost it!"

Jill looked at her young son, fists clenched and face turning red. You've probably experienced just such a moment, where a situation with your child is delicately balanced and is about to turn ugly. Things could still be salvaged and tip toward a good and peaceful resolution. Or they could tilt in the other direction, devolving into chaos, anarchy, even violence.

And it all depends on your little darling controlling an impulse. Calming some big feelings. Making a good decision.

Yikes.

In this case, Jill immediately saw signs of what was coming: Grant was losing control and was *not* going to make a good decision. She saw the fury in his eyes and heard the beginnings of a barbaric growl begin to emerge from his throat. She matched him, step for step, as he raced across the few feet between himself and his sister. Fortunately, Jill was quicker and intercepted Grant before he reached Gracie. She picked him up and held him close as his punches and kicks flailed wildly in the air, Grant screaming all the while. When he finally stopped fighting, Jill set him down. Through his tears he looked at his sister, who actually adored and idolized him, and calmly uttered the phrase, "You're the worst sister in the world."

As Jill told Dan this story, she explained that this last verbal torpedo had hit its mark and produced the dramatic tears from Gracie that Grant had hoped for. Still, Jill was glad that she had been there, or her son likely would have caused physical, not just emotional, pain. The question she asked Dan is one that parents ask us frequently: *I can't be with my kids every second of the day. How do I teach them to do the right thing and control themselves even when I'm not around?*

One of the most important skills we can teach our kids is to make good decisions in high-emotion situations like the one Grant faced here. We want them to pause before acting, to consider consequences, to think about the feelings of others, to make ethical and moral judgments. Sometimes they come through with the kind of behavior that makes us proud. And sometimes they don't.

What is it that makes our kids choose their actions so wisely in certain moments and so poorly in others? Why do certain situations leave us patting our children on the back, and others leave us throwing our hands in the air? Well, there are some pretty good reasons based on what's going on in the higher and lower parts of a child's brain.

THE MENTAL STAIRCASE: INTEGRATING THE UPSTAIRS AND DOWNSTAIRS BRAIN

We can talk about the brain in many ways. In chapter 2, we focused on its two hemispheres, the left and the right. Now we want to look at it from top to bottom, or actually from bottom to top.

Imagine that your brain is a house, with both a downstairs and an upstairs. The downstairs brain includes the brain stem and the limbic region, which are located in the lower parts of the brain, from the top of your neck to about the bridge of your nose. Scientists talk about these lower areas as being more primitive because

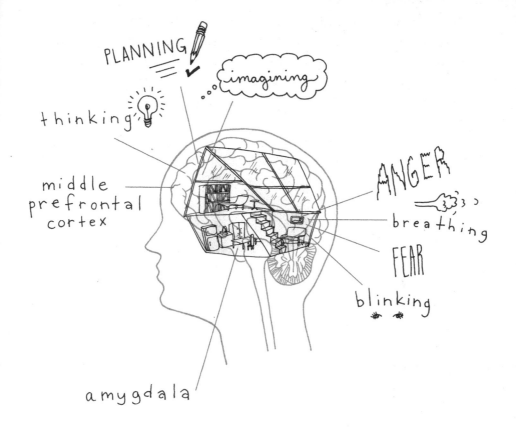

they are responsible for basic functions (like breathing and blinking), for innate reactions and impulses (like fight and flight), and for strong emotions (like anger and fear). Whenever you instinctually flinch because a Little League foul ball flies into the stands, your downstairs brain is doing its job. The same goes for when your face goes red with fury because, after twenty minutes of convincing your kindergartner that the dentist's office won't be scary, the dental assistant enters the room and announces in front of your daughter, "We'll need to give her a shot to numb her." Your anger—along with other strong emotions and bodily functions and instincts—springs from your downstairs brain. It's like the first floor of a house, where so many of a family's basic needs are met. There you'll almost always find a kitchen, a dining room, a bathroom, and so on. Basic necessities get taken care of downstairs.

Your upstairs brain is completely different. It's made up of the cerebral cortex and its various parts—particularly the ones directly behind your forehead, including what's called the middle prefrontal cortex. Unlike your more basic downstairs brain, the upstairs brain is more evolved and can give you a fuller perspective on your world. You might imagine it as a light-filled second-story study or library full of windows and skylights that allow you to see things more clearly. This is where more intricate mental processes take place, like thinking, imagining, and planning. Whereas the downstairs brain is primitive, the upstairs brain is highly sophisticated, controlling some of your most important higher-order and analytical thinking. Because of its sophistication and complexity, it is responsible for producing many of the characteristics we hope to see in our kids:

✓ Sound decision making and planning

✓ Control over emotions and body

✓ Self-understanding

✓ Empathy

✓ Morality

A child whose upstairs brain is properly functioning will demonstrate some of the most important characteristics of a mature and healthy human being. We're not saying she'll be superhuman or never display childish behavior. But when a child's upstairs brain is working well, she can regulate her emotions, consider consequences, think before acting, and consider how others feel—all of which will help her thrive in different areas of her life, as well as help her family survive day-to-day difficulties.

As you might expect, a person's brain works best when the upstairs and downstairs are integrated with each other. So a parent's goal should be to help build and reinforce the metaphorical stairway that connects the child's upper and lower brain so that the two can work as a team. When a fully functioning staircase is in place, the upper and lower parts of the brain are *vertically integrated*. That means that the upstairs can monitor the actions of the downstairs and help calm the strong reactions, impulses, and emotions that originate there. But vertical integration works in the other direction, too, with the downstairs brain and the body (the house's foundation) making important "bottom-up" contributions. After all, we don't want significant upstairs decisions being made in some sort of vacuum that's devoid of input from our emotions, our instincts, and our bodies. Instead, we need to consider our emotional and physical feelings—which originate downstairs—before using the upstairs to decide on a course of action. Once again, then, integration allows for a free flow between the lower and higher parts of our brain. It helps build the stairway, so that all the different parts of our brain can be coordinated and work together as a whole.

THE UNFINISHED UPSTAIRS: SETTING APPROPRIATE EXPECTATIONS FOR YOUR KIDS

Even though we will want to help build this metaphorical staircase in our child's brain, there are two important reasons to maintain realistic expectations when it comes to integration. The first is developmental: while the downstairs brain is well developed even at birth, the upstairs brain isn't fully mature until a person reaches his mid-twenties. In fact, it's one of the last parts of the brain to develop. The upstairs brain remains under massive construction for the first few years of life, then during the teen years undergoes an extensive remodel that lasts into adulthood.

Just imagine the downstairs of a house that is complete and fully furnished, but when you look up at the second floor, you see that it is unfinished and littered with construction tools. You can even see patches of the sky where the roof hasn't been completed yet. That's your child's upstairs brain—a work in progress.

This is really important information for parents to understand, because it means that all of the abilities on the list above—the behaviors and skills we want and expect our kids to demonstrate, like sound decision making, control of their emotions and bodies, empathy, self-understanding, and morality—are dependent on a part of their brain that hasn't fully developed yet. Since the upstairs brain is still under construction, it isn't capable of fully functioning all the time, meaning that it can't be integrated with the downstairs brain and consistently work at its best. As a result, kids are prone to getting "trapped downstairs," without the use of their upstairs brain, which results in them flying off the handle, making poor decisions, and showing a general lack of empathy and self-understanding.

So that's the first reason kids often aren't very good at using the higher and lower parts of the brain together: their upstairs brain is still developing. The other main reason has to do with one particular part of the downstairs brain, the amygdala.

The Baby Gate of the Mind: My Amygdala Made Me Do It

Our amygdala (pronounced *uh-MIG-duh-luh*) is about the size and shape of an almond and is part of the limbic area, which resides in the downstairs brain. The amygdala's job is to quickly process and express emotions, especially anger and fear. This little mass of gray matter is the watchdog of the brain, remaining always alert for times we might be threatened. When it does sense danger, it can completely take over, or hijack, the upstairs brain. That's what allows us to *act* before we *think*. It's the part of the brain that instructs your arm to stretch out to protect your passenger when you're driving and have to stop short. It's the part of the brain that encourages you to scream "Stop!" as was the case when Dan was hiking with his young son, even before he was consciously aware that there was a rattlesnake a few feet up the trail.

Of course, there are definitely times when it's good to act before thinking. In this situation, the last thing Dan needed was to have his upstairs brain go through a series of higher-order maneuvers or perform some sort of cost-benefit analysis: *Oh no! There's a snake up ahead of my son. Now would be a good time to warn him. I wish I had warned him a couple of seconds ago, rather than going through this series of cogitations that led me to the decision to warn him.* Instead, he needed his downstairs brain—in this case, his amygdala—to take over and do exactly what it did: cause him to call out even before he consciously realized what he was doing.

Clearly, acting before thinking is a good thing when we're in a situation like Dan's, or when we're in danger in some other way. But acting or reacting before we think *isn't* usually so good in normal, everyday situations, like when we storm from our car and yell at another parent for breaking the no-waiting rule in the carpool pickup circle. As we'll explain in the "Whole-Brain Kids" section below, that's what we call "flipping our lid," and it's how the amygdala can get us into trouble: it takes over and relieves the upstairs brain from its duties. When we're not truly in danger, we want to think before acting, instead of the other way around.

We want our kids to do the same. The problem, though, is that especially in children, the amygdala frequently fires up and blocks the stairway connecting the upstairs and downstairs brain. It's as if a baby gate has been latched at the bottom of the stairs, making the upstairs brain inaccessible. This of course further compounds the other problem we just discussed: not only is the upstairs brain under construction, but even the part of it that *can* function becomes inaccessible during moments of high emotion or stress.

When your three-year-old erupts in anger because there are no orange Popsicles left in the freezer, his downstairs brain, including the brain stem and amygdala, has sprung into action and latched the baby gate. This primitive part of his brain has received an intense surge of energy, leaving him literally unable to act calmly and reasonably. Massive brain resources have rushed to his downstairs brain, leaving little to power his upstairs brain. As a result, no matter how many times you tell him that you have plenty of purple Popsicles (which he liked better than orange last time anyway), he's probably not going to listen to reason in this moment. He's much more likely to throw something or yell at anyone nearby.

As you know if you've found yourself in this situation, the best way to ease him through this crisis (and in his mind it really *is* a crisis) is to soothe him and help him shift his attention. You might pick him up and show him something else of interest in another room, or you might do something silly or off-the-wall to change the dynamics of the situation. When you do this, you are helping him unlatch the gate, so that the stairway of integration can once again become accessible and he can engage his upstairs brain and begin to calm down.

The same goes for when the problem isn't anger but fear. Think of an active, athletic seven-year-old who refuses to learn to ride a bike. Her amygdala produces such paralyzing fear that she won't even attempt an activity at which she's more than capable of succeeding. Her amygdala has not only placed a baby gate at the bottom of the stairs, it has littered the stairway with the equivalent of balls, skates, books, and shoes—all kinds of obstacles that come from past frightening experiences and make it impossible to reach the higher parts of her brain. In this situation, there would again be many different possible strategies for clearing the pathway. Her parents might try to persuade her of the reward of taking on a new challenge; they might acknowledge and discuss their own fears; they might even offer an incentive to help her conquer her fear. Any number of approaches might work to help her clear the connection to her upstairs brain and quiet her amygdala, which is shouting the message that she might fall and hurt herself.

Think about what this information means, practically, as we raise kids who don't have constant access to their upstairs brain. It's unrealistic to expect them always to be rational, regulate their emotions, make good decisions, think before acting, and be empathetic—all of the things a developed upstairs brain helps them do. They can demonstrate some of these qualities to varying degrees much of the time, depending on their age. But for the most part, kids just don't have the biological skill set to do so *all* the time. Sometimes they can use their upstairs brain, and sometimes they can't. Just knowing this and adjusting our expectations can help us see that our kids are often doing the best they can with the brain they have.

So does that give them a get-out-of-jail-free card ("Sorry, Mom, that I squirted our new puppy's face with Windex. I guess my upstairs brain wasn't fully engaged")? Hardly. In fact, it actually gives us parents even more incentive to see that our kids develop the faculties that result in *appropriate* behavior. And it gives us a pretty effective strategy for making some dicey decisions, especially when we're in the middle of a heated situation—like a tantrum.

TANTRUMS: UPSTAIRS AND DOWNSTAIRS

The dreaded tantrum can be one of the most unpleasant parts of parenting. Whether it takes place in private or in public, it can, in the blink of an eye, turn the person who owns our heart and moves mountains with one beautiful little smile, into the most unattractive and repulsive being on the planet.

Most parents have been taught that there's only one good way to respond to a tantrum: ignore it. Otherwise, you communicate to your child that she has a powerful weapon to wield against you, and she will wield it over and over again.

But what does this new knowledge about the brain say about tantrums? When you know about the upstairs and downstairs brain, you can also see that there are really two different types of tantrums. An *upstairs tantrum* occurs when a child essentially *decides* to throw a fit. She makes a conscious choice to act out, to push buttons and terrorize you until she get what she wants. Despite her dramatic and seemingly heartfelt pleas, she could instantly stop the tantrum if she wanted to—for instance, if you gave in to her demands or reminded her that she is about to lose a cherished privilege. The reason she can stop is that she is using her upstairs brain at that moment. She is *able* to control her emotions and body, to be logical and make good decisions. She may look like she's completely out of control as she screams in the middle of the mall, "I want those princess slippers *now!*" But you can see that she knows what she's doing, and that she's definitely working from strategy and manipulation to achieve a desired end: that you drop everything and immediately buy the slippers.

A parent who recognizes an upstairs tantrum is left with one clear response: never negotiate with a terrorist. An upstairs tantrum calls for firm boundaries and a clear discussion about appropriate and inappropriate behavior. A good response in this situation would be to calmly explain, "I understand that you're excited about the slippers, but I don't like the way you're acting. If you don't stop now, you won't get the slippers, and I'll need to cancel your playdate this afternoon, because you're showing me that you're not able to handle yourself well." Then it's important to follow through on those consequences if the behavior doesn't stop. By providing this type of firm limit, you're giving your daughter practice at seeing the consequences of her inappropriate actions, and at learning to control her impulses. You're teaching her that respectful communication, patience, and delayed gratification pay off—and that contrary behaviors don't. Important lessons for a developing brain.

If you refuse to give in to upstairs tantrums—regardless of the age of your child—you'll stop seeing them on a regular basis. Since upstairs tantrums are intentional, children will stop returning to that particular strategy when they learn that it's ineffective—and often even leads to negative results.

A *downstairs tantrum* is completely different. Here, a child becomes so upset that he's no longer *able* to use his upstairs brain. Your toddler becomes so angry that you poured water on his head to wash his hair that he begins screaming, throwing toys out of the tub, and wildly swinging his fists, trying to hit you. In this case, the lower parts of his brain—in particular his amygdala—take over and hijack his upstairs brain. He's not even close to being in a state of integration. In fact, the stress hormones flooding his little body mean that virtually no part of his higher brain is fully functioning. As a result, he's literally incapable—momentarily, at least—of controlling his body or emotions, and of using all of those higher-order thinking skills, like considering consequences, solving problems, or considering others' feelings. He's flipped his lid. The baby gate is blocking access to the upstairs, and he simply can't use his whole brain. (When you later tell someone that your child "totally lost his mind," you'll actually be more neurologically accurate than you realize!)

When your child is in this state of dis-integration and a full-blown downstairs tantrum has erupted, a completely different parental response is called for. Whereas a child throwing an upstairs tantrum needs a parent to quickly set firm boundaries, an appropriate response to a downstairs tantrum is much more nurturing and comforting. As in the "connect and redirect" technique we discussed in chapter 2, the first thing a parent needs to do is to connect with the child and help him calm himself down. This can often be accomplished through loving touch and a soothing tone of voice. Or, if he has gone so far that he's in danger of hurting himself or someone else or destroying property, you may have to hold him close and calmly talk him down as you remove him from the scene.

You can experiment with different approaches depending on your child's temperament, but what's most important is that you help soothe him and steer him away from the chaos bank of the river. There's no sense in talking about consequences or appropriate behavior. He simply can't process any of that information when he's in the middle of his downstairs tantrum, because that conversation requires a functioning upstairs brain that can listen and assimilate information. So your first task, when your child's upstairs brain has been hijacked by his downstairs brain, is to help calm his amygdala.

Then, once the upstairs brain reenters the picture, you can begin to respond to the issue using logic and reason. ("Did you not like it that Daddy washed your hair like that? Do you have any ideas about how we should wash your hair next time?") Once he is in a more receptive place, you can also talk about appropriate and inappropriate behavior, and about any possible consequences ("I know you were really angry about the water splashing in your face. But it's not OK to hit when you're mad. You can use words and tell Daddy, 'I don't like that. Please stop' "). Your discipline can now maintain your authority—that's crucial—but you can do so from a more informed and compassionate position. And your child is more likely to internalize the lesson because you're teaching it when his brain is more receptive to learning.

As any veteran parent knows, flipping the lid isn't unique to toddlers. It may look different when it occurs in a ten-year-old, but a child of any age (or even an adult!) is prone to having the downstairs brain take over in high-emotion situations. That's why an awareness of the upstairs brain and the downstairs brain—and the tantrums that originate from each place—can help us be much more effective as we discipline our children. We can more clearly see when it's time to draw the line and when it's time to bring lots of nurturing compassion to help engage the upstairs brain.

Tantrums provide just one example of how practical this upstairs-downstairs knowledge can be. Now let's talk about other ways you can help develop your child's upstairs brain and allow it to become stronger and more integrated with the downstairs brain.

What You Can Do:
Helping Develop and Integrate Your Child's Upstairs Brain

Whole-Brain Strategy #3:
Engage, Don't Enrage: Appealing to the Upstairs Brain

Ask yourself, as you interact with your kids through the day, which part of their brain you're appealing to. Are you engaging the upstairs? Or are you triggering the downstairs? The answer to this question can go a long way toward determining the outcome of one of those delicately balanced parenting moments. Here's a story Tina tells about a time she faced just such a moment with her son:

> While eating at one of our favorite Mexican restaurants, I noticed that my four-year-old had left the table and was standing behind a pillar about ten feet away. As much as I love him, and as adorable as he is most of the time, when I saw his angry, defiant face coupled with his repeated tongue-thrusting aimed at our table, "adorable" wasn't the word that came to my mind. A few diners at surrounding tables noticed and looked at my husband, Scott, and me to see how we were going to handle the situation. In that moment, Scott and I felt the pressure and judgment of those watching and expecting us to lay down the law about manners at a restaurant.
>
> I clearly saw two choices as I walked over and crouched down eye-level with my son. Option #1: I could go the traditional "command and demand" route and open with a clichéd threat uttered in a stern tone: "Stop making faces, young man. Go sit down and eat your lunch or you won't get any dessert."
>
> At times option #1 might be an appropriate parental response. But for my little guy, this verbal and nonverbal con-

frontation would have triggered all kinds of reactive emotions in his downstairs brain—the part scientists call the reptilian brain— and he would have fought back like a reptile under attack.

Or option #2: I could tap into his upstairs brain in an effort to get more of a thinking—as opposed to a fighting/reacting— response.

Now, I make plenty of mistakes as I parent my boys (as they'll freely tell you). But just the day before, I had given a lecture to a group of parents about the upstairs and downstairs brain, and about using everyday challenges—the survival moments—as opportunities to help our kids thrive. So, luckily for my son, all of that was fresh in my mind. I decided to choose option #2.

I started with an observation: "You look like you feel angry. Is that right?" (Remember "connect and redirect"?) He scrunched up his face in ferocity, stuck out his tongue again, and loudly proclaimed, "Yes!" I was actually relieved that he stopped there; it wouldn't have been at all unlike him to add his latest favorite insult and call me "Fart-face Jones." (I swear I don't know where they learn this stuff.)

I asked him what he felt angry about and discovered that he was furious that Scott had told him he needed to eat at least half of his quesadilla before he could have dessert. I explained that I could see why that would be disappointing, and I said, "Well, Daddy's really good at negotiating. Decide what you think would be a fair amount to eat, and then go talk to him about it. Let me know if you need help coming up with your plan." I tousled his hair, returned to the table, and watched his once-again adorable face show evidence of doing some hard thinking. His upstairs brain was definitely engaged. In fact, it was at war with his downstairs brain. So far we had avoided a blow-up, but it still felt like a dangerous fuse might be burning within him.

Within fifteen seconds or so, my son returned and said to Scott in an angry tone of voice, "Dad, I don't want to eat half of my quesadilla. *And* I want dessert." Scott's response perfectly dovetailed with my own: "Well, what do you think would be a fair amount?"

The answer came with slow, firm resolve: "I've got one word for you: Ten bites."

What makes this unmathematical response even funnier is that ten bites meant that he would eat well over half the quesadilla. So Scott accepted the counteroffer, my son happily gobbled down ten bites and then his dessert, and the whole family (as well as the restaurant's other patrons) got to enjoy lunch with no further incidents. My son's downstairs brain never fully took over, which, luckily for us, meant that his upstairs brain had won the day.

Again, option #1 would have been perfectly fine, even appropriate. But it also would have missed an opportunity. My son would have missed a chance to see that relationships are about connection, communication, and compromise. He would have missed a chance to feel empowered that he can make choices, affect his environment, and solve problems. In short, he would have missed an opportunity to exercise and develop his upstairs brain.

And I hasten to point out that even though I chose option #2, Scott and I still had to address the misbehavior part of the incident. Once our son was more in control of himself and could actually be receptive to what we had to say, we discussed the importance of being respectful and using good manners in a restaurant, even when he's unhappy.

This is an example of how simple awareness of the downstairs and upstairs brain can have a direct and immediate impact on the way we parent and discipline our children. Notice that when the challenge arose, Tina asked herself, "Which part of the brain do I want to appeal to here?" She could have gotten what she wanted by challenging her son and demanding that he change his behavior immediately. She has enough authority in his eyes that he would have obeyed (albeit resentfully). But that approach would have triggered the downstairs brain, and his anger and feelings of unfairness would have raged within him. So instead, Tina engaged his upstairs brain by helping him think through the situation and find a way to negotiate with his father.

Let's make one thing clear: sometimes there is no place for negotiation in parent-child interactions. Children need to respect their parents' authority, and sometimes that means that no simply means no, without wiggle room. Also, sometimes counteroffers

STRATEGY #3

INSTEAD OF ENRAGING THE DOWNSTAIRS BRAIN...

...ENGAGE THE UPSTAIRS BRAIN

are unacceptable. If Tina's four-year-old had suggested that he take only one bite of his lunch, his dad wouldn't have been open to striking that particular deal.

But as we parent and discipline our kids, we are given *so many* opportunities to interact in ways that engage and develop their upstairs brain.

Notice how, in the illustration on page 51, the mother chose *not* to present an ultimatum that would enrage the downstairs brain. Instead, she engaged the upstairs brain by first directing her daughter to use more precise and specific words for how she was feeling ("Are you feeling really mad because I didn't get you that necklace?"). Then she asked her daughter to work with her to be a problem solver. Once the girl asks, "How do we do that?" the mother knows that the upstairs brain is engaged. Her daughter is now able to discuss the issue with her mom in a way she couldn't just a few seconds ago. Now they can brainstorm together about getting another necklace at the store or making one at home. The mother can also now talk to her daughter about how to use her words when she's angry.

Every time we say "Convince me" or "Come up with a solution that works for both of us," we give our kids the chance to practice problem solving and decision making. We help them consider appropriate behaviors and consequences, and we help them think about what another person feels and wants. All because we found a way to engage the upstairs, instead of enraging the downstairs.

Whole-Brain Strategy #4:
Use It or Lose It: Exercising the Upstairs Brain

In addition to appealing to our children's upstairs brain, we also want to help them exercise it. The upstairs brain is like a muscle: when it gets used, it develops, gets stronger, and performs better. And when it gets ignored, it doesn't develop optimally, losing some of its power and ability to function. That's what we mean by "use it or lose it." We want to be intentional about developing the upstairs brain of our children. As we've been saying, a strong upstairs brain balances out the downstairs brain, and is essential for social and emotional intelligence. It's the foundation of solid mental health. Our job is to provide our kids with opportunity after opportunity to exercise their upstairs brain so that it can grow stronger and more powerful.

As you and your children go through your day, watch for ways you can focus on and exercise different functions of the upstairs brain. Let's look at a few of them, one by one.

Sound Decision Making

One big parental temptation is to make decisions for our kids, so that they consistently do the right thing. But as often as possible, we need to give them practice at making decisions for themselves. Decision making requires what's called executive functioning, which occurs when the upstairs brain weighs different options. Considering several competing alternatives, as well as the outcomes of those choices, gives a child's upstairs brain practice, strengthening it and allowing it to work better.

For very young children, this can be as simple as asking, "Do you want to wear your blue shoes or your white shoes today?" Then, as kids get older, we can give them more responsibility in the decision making and allow them to take on some dilemmas that can really challenge them. For instance, if your ten-year-old daughter has a scheduling conflict—both her Girl Scout campout and her soccer playoff are on Saturday and she clearly can't be in both places at the same time—encourage her to make the choice. She's much more likely to be comfortable, if not completely happy, about having to give up one commitment if she's been a part of the process of making the decision.

An allowance is another terrific way to give older kids practice at dealing with difficult dilemmas. The experience of deciding between buying a computer game now or continuing to save for that new bike is a powerful way to exercise the upstairs brain. The point is to let your children wrestle with the decision and live with the consequences. Whenever you can do so responsibly, avoid solving and resist rescuing, even when they make minor mistakes or not-so-great choices. After all, your goal here isn't perfection on every decision right now, but an optimally developed upstairs brain down the road.

Controlling Emotions and the Body

Another important—and difficult—task for little ones is to remain in control of themselves. So we need to give them skills that help them make good decisions when they are upset. Use the techniques you're probably already familiar with: Teach them to take a deep breath, or count to ten. Help them express their feelings. Let them stomp their feet or punch a pillow. You can also teach them what's happening in their brains when they feel themselves losing control—and how to avoid "flipping their lid." (We'll help you with this in the "Whole-Brain Kids" section at the end of the chapter.)

Even small children have the capacity to stop and think instead of hurting someone with their words or their fists. They won't always make good decisions, but the more fully they practice alternatives other than lashing out, the stronger and more capable their upstairs brain will become.

Self-understanding

One of the best ways to foster self-understanding in your children is to ask questions that help them look beyond the surface of what they understand: *Why do you think you made that choice? What made you feel that way? Why do you think you didn't do well on your test—was it because you were hurrying, or is this just really difficult material?*

This is what one father did for his ten-year-old, Catherine, as he helped her pack for camp. He asked whether she expected to feel homesick while she was away. When he received the expected noncommittal "Maybe" in response, he followed up with another question: "How do you think you'll handle that?"

Again he received a non-answer—"I don't know"—but this time he could see her beginning to think about the question, if only a little.

So he pressed further: "If you do start feeling homesick, what's something you can do to feel better?"

Catherine continued stuffing clothes into her duffel bag, but she was obviously thinking about the question now. Finally she offered an actual answer: "I guess I could write you a letter, or I could do something fun with my friends."

From here she and her father were able to talk for a couple of minutes about her expectations and concerns about going away, and she developed a bit more self-understanding. Simply because her father asked her a few questions.

When your child is old enough to be able to write—or even just draw—you might give him a journal and encourage daily writing or drawing. This ritual can enhance his ability to pay attention to and understand his internal landscape. Or for a younger child, have her draw pictures that tell a story. The more your kids think about what's going on within themselves, the more they will develop the ability to understand and respond to what's going on in the worlds within and around them.

Empathy

Empathy is another important function of the upstairs brain. When you ask simple questions that encourage the consideration of another's feelings, you are building your child's ability to feel empathy. At a restaurant: "Why do you think that baby is crying?" While you're reading together: "How do you think Melinda is feeling now that her friend moved away?" Leaving the store: "That woman wasn't very nice to us, was she? Do you think something might have happened to her that made her feel sad today?"

Simply by drawing your child's attention to other people's emotions during everyday encounters, you can open up whole new levels of compassion within them and exercise their upstairs brain. Scientists are beginning more and more to think that empathy has its roots in a complex system of what are being called mirror neurons, which we'll discuss in the next chapter. The more you give your child's upstairs brain practice at thinking of others, the more capable he will be of having compassion.

INSTEAD OF JUST GIVING THE ANSWER...

...EXERCISE THE UPSTAIRS BRAIN

Morality

All of the above attributes of a well-integrated upstairs brain culminate in one of our most important goals for our children: a strong sense of morality. When kids can make sound decisions while controlling themselves and working from empathy and self-understanding, they will develop a robust and active sense of morality, a sense of not only right and wrong, but also what is for the greater good beyond their own individual needs. Again, we can't expect absolute consistency because of their still-developing brain. But we do want to raise questions regarding morals and ethics as often as possible in normal, everyday situations.

Another way to exercise this part of the brain is to offer hypothetical situations, which kids often love: *Would it be OK to run a red light if there was an emergency? If a bully was picking on someone at school and there were no adults around, what would you do?* The point is to challenge your children to think about how they act, and to consider the implications of their decisions. In doing so, you give your kids practice thinking through moral and ethical principles, which, with your guidance, will become the foundation for the way they make decisions for the rest of their lives.

And, of course, consider what you are modeling with your own behavior. As you teach them about honesty, generosity, kindness, and respect, make sure that they see you living a life that embodies those values as well. The examples you set, for good and for bad, will significantly impact the way your child's upstairs brain develops.

Whole-Brain Strategy #5:
Move It or Lose It: Moving the Body to Avoid
Losing the Mind

Research has shown that bodily movement directly affects brain chemistry. So when one of your children has lost touch with his upstairs brain, a powerful way to help him regain balance is to have him move his body. Here's a story a mother told us about her ten-year-old son and a time he regained control by being physically active.

Two days after Liam started fifth grade, he felt completely overwhelmed by the amount of homework his teacher had assigned. (I agreed with him, by the way. It was a lot.) He was complaining about it, but he eventually went to his room to work on it.

When I went to check on his progress, I found him literally curled up in a fetal position under his bean bag chair in his room. I encouraged him to come out, to sit at his desk and keep working on his studies. He kept whining, saying he couldn't do it: "It's just too much!" I kept offering to help him, and he kept refusing my help.

Then all of a sudden, he jumped out from under the bean bag chair, ran downstairs, ran out the front door, and kept running. He ran several blocks through the neighborhood before coming home.

When we had him safely back in the house, and he had calmed down and had a snack, I was able to talk with him and ask why he had taken off like that. He said he didn't really know. He said, "The only thing I can think of is that I felt like it would make me feel better if I ran as fast as I could for as long as I could. And it did." And I have to admit—he did seem a lot more calm, and ready to have me help him with his homework.

Even though Liam didn't know it, when he left the house and ran, he was practicing integration. His downstairs brain had bullied his upstairs brain into submission, leaving him feeling overwhelmed and helpless. He had floated way over near the chaos bank of the river. His mother's attempts to help bring in his upstairs brain were unsuccessful, but when Liam brought his body into the conversation, something changed in his brain. After a few minutes of exercise, he was able to calm his amygdala and give control back to his upstairs brain.

Studies support Liam and his spontaneous strategy. Research shows that when we change our physical state—through movement or relaxation, for example—we can change our emotional state. Try smiling for a minute—it can make you feel happier; quick, shallow breaths accompany anxiety, and if you take a slow, deep breath, you'll likely feel calmer. (You can try these little exercises with your child to teach her how her body affects how she feels.)

The body is full of information that it sends to the brain. In fact, a lot of the emotion we feel actually begins in the body. Our churning stomach and tense shoulders send physical messages of anxiety to the brain before we even consciously realize that we're nervous. The flow of energy and information from the body up into our brain stem, into our limbic region, and then up into the cortex, changes our bodily states, our emotional states, and our thoughts.

What happened for Liam, then, was that the movement of his body helped bring his whole self into a state of integration, so his upstairs brain, his downstairs brain, and his body could all once again do their jobs in a way that was effective and healthy. When he felt overwhelmed, the flow of energy and information became blocked, resulting in dis-integration. Vigorously moving his body released some of his angry energy and tension, allowing him to relax. So after his run, his body sent "calmer" information to his upstairs brain, meaning that his emotional balance returned and the different parts of his brain and body began to function again in an integrated way.

The next time your children need help calming down or regaining control, look for ways to get them moving. For young kids, experiment with what might be called creative, loving trickery, as shown on page 60.

The fun of this game, coupled with the physical activity, can completely change your toddler's mind-set and make the whole morning much more enjoyable for both of you.

This technique works for older kids, also. A Little League coach we know heard about the "move it or lose it" principle and ended up having his players jump up and down in the dugout when they got discouraged after giving up a few early runs during the championship. The boys' movement brought a shift of excitement and new energy into their bodies and brains, and they eventually came back and won the game. (Chalk up another victory for neuroscience!)

INSTEAD OF COMMAND AND DEMAND...

...TRY MOVE IT OR LOSE IT

At times, too, you can simply explain the concept: *I know you're mad you didn't get to go on the sleepover with your sister. Doesn't seem fair, does it? Let's go ride our bikes and talk about it. Sometimes just moving your body can help your brain feel like things are going to be OK.* However you do it, the point is to help your child regain some sort of balance and control by moving their body, which can remove blockages and pave the way for integration to return.

Whole-Brain Kids:
Teach Your Kids About Their Downstairs and Upstairs Brain

Kids can pretty easily understand the upstairs-downstairs information we've presented in this chapter. Here's something you can read to your child to help get the conversation going.

YOUR DOWNSTAIRS BRAIN AND YOUR UPSTAIRS BRAIN

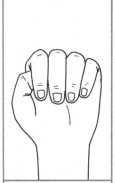

MAKE A FIST WITH YOUR HAND. THIS IS WHAT WE CALL A HAND MODEL OF YOUR BRAIN. REMEMBER HOW YOU HAVE A LEFT SIDE AND A RIGHT SIDE TO YOUR BRAIN? WELL, YOU ALSO HAVE AN UPSTAIRS AND A DOWN-STAIRS PART OF YOUR BRAIN.

THE UPSTAIRS BRAIN IS WHERE YOU MAKE GOOD DECISIONS AND DO THE RIGHT THING, EVEN WHEN YOU ARE FEELING REALLY UPSET.

NOW LIFT YOUR FINGERS A LITTLE BIT. SEE WHERE YOUR THUMB IS? THAT'S PART OF YOUR DOWN-STAIRS BRAIN, AND IT'S WHERE YOUR REALLY BIG FEELINGS COME FROM. IT LETS YOU CARE ABOUT OTHER PEOPLE AND FEEL LOVE. IT ALSO LETS YOU FEEL UPSET, LIKE WHEN YOU'RE MAD OR FRUS-TRATED.

THERE'S NOTHING WRONG WITH FEELING UPSET. THAT'S NORMAL, ESPECIALLY WHEN YOUR UPSTAIRS BRAIN HELPS YOU CALM DOWN. FOR EXAMPLE, CLOSE YOUR FINGERS AGAIN. SEE HOW THE UPSTAIRS THINKING PART OF YOUR BRAIN IS TOUCHING YOUR THUMB, SO IT CAN HELP YOUR DOWNSTAIRS BRAIN EXPRESS YOUR FEELINGS CALMLY?

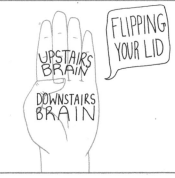

SOMETIMES WHEN WE GET REALLY UPSET, WE CAN FLIP OUR LID. RAISE YOUR FINGERS LIKE THIS. SEE HOW YOUR UPSTAIRS BRAIN IS NO LONGER TOUCHING YOUR DOWNSTAIRS BRAIN? THAT MEANS IT CAN'T HELP IT STAY CALM.

FOR EXAMPLE:

THIS IS WHAT HAPPENED TO JEFFREY WHEN HIS SISTER DESTROYED HIS LEGO TOWER. HE FLIPPED HIS LID AND WANTED TO SCREAM AT HER.

BUT JEFFREY'S PARENTS HAD TAUGHT HIM ABOUT FLIPPING HIS LID, AND HOW HIS UPSTAIRS BRAIN COULD HUG HIS DOWN-STAIRS BRAIN AND HELP HIM CALM DOWN. HE WAS STILL ANGRY, BUT INSTEAD OF SHOUTING AT HIS SISTER, HE WAS ABLE TO TELL HER HE WAS ANGRY AND ASK HIS PARENTS TO TAKE HER OUT OF HIS ROOM.

SO THE NEXT TIME YOU FEEL YOURSELF STARTING TO FLIP YOUR LID, MAKE A BRAIN MODEL WITH YOUR HAND. (REMEMBER, IT'S A BRAIN MODEL, NOT AN ANGRY FIST!) PUT YOUR FINGERS STRAIGHT UP, THEN SLOWLY LOWER THEM SO THAT THEY'RE HUGGING YOUR THUMB. THIS WILL BE YOUR REMINDER TO USE YOUR UPSTAIRS BRAIN TO HELP YOU CALM THOSE BIG FEELINGS FROM THE DOWNSTAIRS BRAIN.

Integrating Ourselves: Using Our Own Mental Staircase

"My young son was screaming for forty-five minutes and I didn't know how to comfort him. I finally screamed back, 'Sometimes I hate you!' "

"My son was two and scratched his baby brother's face so hard that he left marks. I spanked his bottom, like five hard swats. Then I left the room, walked down the hall, turned back around, and spanked him probably five more swats again. I screamed at him so loud, I terrified him."

"After I had told my daughter to watch out for her little brother running in front of the swing, she almost swung right into him. I was so mad that even in front of other people at the park I said to her, 'What's wrong with you—are you stupid?' "

These are some pretty awful parenting experiences, aren't they? They represent our downstairs moments, the times when we're so out of control that we say or do something we'd never let anyone else say or do to our child.

The confessions above come from real parents whom we know personally. And although it may surprise you, each of those parents does a great job at raising their kids. But like the rest of us, they just lose it from time to time and say and do things they wish they hadn't.

Could you add your own downstairs moment to the list above? Of course you could. You're a parent, and you're human. We see it time and again when we speak to and counsel parents: in high-stress parenting situations, parents make mistakes. All of us do.

But don't forget: parenting crises are openings for growth and integration. You can use the moments when you feel yourself losing control as opportunities to model self-regulation. Little eyes are watching to see how *you* calm *yourself* down. Your actions set an example of how to make a good choice in a high-emotion moment when you're in danger of flipping *your* lid.

So what do you do when you recognize that your downstairs brain has taken over and you've begun to lose your mind? First, do no harm. Close your mouth to avoid saying something you'll regret. Put your hands behind your back to avoid any kind of rough physical contact. When you're in a downstairs moment, protect your child at all costs.

Second, remove yourself from the situation and collect yourself. There's nothing wrong with taking a breather, especially when it means protecting your child. You can tell her you need a break to calm down so she doesn't feel rejected. Then, although it might feel a bit silly at times, try out the "move it or lose it" technique. Do jumping jacks. Try some yoga stretches. Take slow, deep breaths. Do whatever it takes to regain some of the control you lost when your amygdala hijacked your upstairs brain. You'll not only move into a more integrated state yourself, but also model for your kids some quick self-regulation tricks they can use.

Finally, repair. Quickly. Reconnect with your child as soon as you are calm and feeling more in control of yourself. Then deal with whatever emotional and relational harm has been done. This may involve your expressing forgiveness, but it may also require that you apologize and accept responsibility for your own actions. This step needs to occur as quickly as possible. The sooner you repair the connection between yourself and your child, the sooner you can both regain your emotional balance and get back to enjoying your relationship together.

CHAPTER 4

Kill the Butterflies!

Integrating Memory for Growth and Healing

"There is no way I'm taking swimming lessons this summer!"

Tina's seven-year-old made this firm proclamation when he found out his parents had signed him up for lessons at their local high school pool. Sitting at the dinner table, he glared at his mom and dad, setting his jaw and narrowing his eyes.

Tina looked to her husband, Scott, who shrugged, as if to say, *OK, I'll go first.*

"I don't get it. You love swimming."

"*Exactly,* Dad, that's the *point.*" He even sounded sarcastic. "I already *know* how to swim."

Scott nodded. "We know you do. The lessons are to help you get better."

Tina added, "Plus Henry's doing it. You'll be hanging out with him every day next week."

He shook his head. "No way. I don't care." He looked down at his plate, and a hint of fear crept into his determined voice. "Please don't make me do this."

Scott and Tina exchanged a look and said they'd think about it and continue the discussion later. But they were shocked. It was absolutely unheard of for their son to turn down any activity with Henry, his best friend, especially one related to athletics.

Situations like this come up all the time for parents, where they are left completely baffled by the way their child responds to something they say. When fear, anger, frustration, and other big emotions overpower children and they act in ways that don't make sense, there may be an easily fixable reason. They may simply be hungry or tired. Or maybe they've been in the car too long. Or maybe it's just because they're two (or three, or four, or five—or fifteen). But other times, a child acts out or behaves uncharacteristically because of more deep-seated reasons.

For example, as Tina and Scott spoke later that night, they agreed that their son's surprising right-brained response likely resulted from a mildly traumatic experience he had undergone three years earlier, an experience he probably wasn't even thinking about. Tina knew this was a great time to introduce her son to a couple of important facts about the brain, so at bedtime that night, that's what she did. Before we tell you about that conversation, we should first explain what Tina was trying to accomplish when she talked to her son. She knew that one of the best ways to help a child deal with difficult experiences is to understand some basics about the science of how memory works in the brain.

Memory and the Brain: A Couple of Myths

Let's start with two myths about memory.

> *Myth #1: Memory is a mental file cabinet. When you think back about your first date or the birth of your child, you just open the appropriate file drawer in your brain and call up that memory.*

It would be nice and convenient if this were true, but that's just not the way the brain works. There aren't thousands of little "memory files" in your head waiting for you to access them and bring them to consciousness so you can think about them. Instead, memory is all about associations. As an association machine, the brain processes something in the present moment—an idea, a feeling, a smell, an image—and links that experience with similar experiences from the past. These past experiences strongly influence how we understand what we see or feel. That influence occurs because of associations in the brain, where different neurons (or brain cells) become linked to each other. So, in essence, memory is the way an event from the past influences us in the present.

Imagine, for example, that you found an old pacifier between your couch cushions. What kind of emotions and memories would you experience? If you still have a baby in the house, maybe nothing too earth-shattering. But if it's been a few years since your little one used a pacifier, then you might be flooded with sentimental associations. You might remember how giant it looked in your newborn's mouth, or how quickly you moved the first time your toddler shared the binky with the dog. Or you might relive that wretched night when you all said goodbye to pacifiers for good. In the moment that you find the pacifier, all kinds of associations rush back into your awareness, impacting your present feelings and mood based on strong associations from the past. This is what memory essentially is—association.

Without getting too complicated, here's what goes on in the brain. Anytime we undergo an experience, neurons "fire," or become activated with electrical signals. When these brain cells fire, they become linked with or join other neurons. These linkages create associations. As we explained in the introduction, this means that every experience literally changes the physical makeup of the brain, since neurons are constantly being connected (and separated) based on our experiences. Neuroscientists explain this process with the phrase "Neurons that fire together wire together." In other words, every new experience causes certain neurons to fire, and when they do, they wire together, or link up, with other neurons that are firing at the same time.

Doesn't this fit with your experience? The very mention of biting into a lemon can make you salivate. Or a song in the car transports you back to an awkward slow dance in high school.

Or remember when you gave your four-year-old a piece of bubble gum after ballet class that one time? And what did she want and expect after every ballet class from then on? Of course. Bubble gum. Why? Because her end-of-ballet-class neurons had fired and wired with her bubble-gum neurons. Neurons that fire together wire together.

That's how memory works. One experience (the end of ballet class) causes certain neurons to fire, and those neurons can get wired to neurons from another experience (getting bubble gum). Then each time we undergo the first experience, our brain connects it with the second one. Thus, when ballet ends, our brain triggers an expectation of getting gum. The trigger might be an internal event—a thought or a feeling—or an external event that the brain associates with something from your past. Regardless, this triggered memory then sets up expectations for the future. The brain continually prepares itself for the future based on what happened before. Memories shape our current perceptions by causing us to anticipate what will happen next. Our past absolutely shapes our present and future. And it does so via associations within the brain.

> *Myth #2: Memory is like a photocopy machine. When you call up memories, you see accurate, exact reproductions of what took place in the past. You remember yourself on your first date with ridiculous hair and clothes, and you laugh at your own nervousness. Or you see the doctor holding up your newborn and you relive the intense emotions of that moment.*

Again, that's not quite how it happens. Well, the ridiculous hair and clothes may have really happened, but memory is not an exact reproduction of events from your past. Whenever you retrieve a memory, you alter it. What you recall may be close to exactly what happened, but the very act of recalling an experience changes it, sometimes in significant ways. To put it scientifically, memory retrieval activates a neural cluster similar to, but not identical with, the one created at the time of encoding. Thus memories are distorted—sometimes slightly, sometimes greatly—even though you believe you are being accurate.

You've had those conversations with your sibling or your

spouse where after you tell a story about something, they say "That's not how it happened!" Your state of mind when you encoded the memory and the state of mind you're in when you recall it influence and change the memory itself. So the story you actually tell is less history and more historical fiction.

Keep these two myths in mind as we talk in the following pages about your kids and the way their past experiences impact them. Remember that memory is all about linkages in the brain (as opposed to being alphabetical files to be accessed whenever needed), and that retrieved memories are by definition vulnerable to distortion (as opposed to being detail-for-detail accurate photocopies from your past).

THE TRUTH ABOUT MEMORY: LET'S GET EXPLICIT (AND IMPLICIT)

Think about your memory for changing a diaper. When you approach a changing table, you don't actively talk yourself through the process: "OK, first place the baby on the pad. Now unzip the pajamas and remove the soggy diaper. Place the clean diaper under the baby and . . ."

No, none of that's necessary because when you change a diaper, you just do it. You've done it so many times before, you don't even think about what you're doing. Your brain fires off clusters of neurons that let you undo the tabs, remove the diaper, reach for a baby wipe, and so on, all without ever even realizing that you are "remembering" how to do it. That's one kind of memory: past experiences (changing diaper after diaper) influence your behavior in the present (changing this particular diaper) without any realization that your memory has even been triggered.

If, on the other hand, you think about that day you first changed a diaper, you might pause for a moment, scan your memory, and come up with an image of yourself nervously gripping a baby's ankle, then cringing at the mess you find in the diaper, then struggling to figure out what to do next. When you actively think about these images and emotions, then you're aware that you are recalling something from the past. This is also memory—but it's different from the memory that enables you to change a diaper now without thinking about it.

These two types of memory interweave and work together in your normal everyday living. The memory that enables you to change your baby without knowing that you are remembering is called *implicit memory*. Your ability to recall learning to change a diaper (or to recall any other specific moment) is *explicit memory*. Usually when we talk about memory, we mean what is technically explicit memory: a conscious recollection of a past experience. But we need to know about both kinds of memory, for our own sake as well as for that of our children. By getting a clear handle on these two different types of memory, we can provide our kids with what they need as they grow and mature and deal with difficult experiences.

Let's start by focusing on implicit memories, which begin forming even before we are born. Dan tells a story about an informal "research study" he performed in his own family.

> When my wife was pregnant with each of our two children, I used to sing to them in the womb. It was an old Russian song that my grandmother had sung to me, a child's song about her love for life and for her mother—"May there always be sunshine, may there always be good times, may there always be Mama, and may there always be me." I sang it—in Russian and in English—during the last trimester of pregnancy, when I knew the auditory system was wired up enough to register sound coming through the amniotic fluid.
>
> Then in the first week after each child was born, I invited a colleague over for a "research study." (I know, it wasn't controlled, but it was fun.) Without revealing the prenatal song, I sang three different songs in turn. No doubt about it—when the babies heard the familiar song, their eyes opened wider and they became more alert, so that my colleague could easily identify the change in their attention level. A perceptual memory had been encoded. (Now my kids won't let me sing; I probably sounded better underwater.)

Dan's newborn children recognized his voice and the Russian song because that information had been encoded in their brain as implicit memories. We encode implicit memory throughout our lives, and in the first eighteen months we encode *only* implicitly. An infant encodes the smells and tastes and sounds of home and parents, the sensations in her belly when she's hungry, the bliss of warm milk, the way her mother's body stiffens in response to a certain relative's arrival. Implicit memory encodes our perceptions, our emotions, our bodily sensations, and, as we get older, behaviors like learning to crawl and walk and ride a bike and eventually change a diaper.

What's crucial to understand about implicit memory—especially when it comes to our kids and their fears and frustrations—is that implicit memories cause us to form expectations about the way the world works, based on our previous experiences. Remember the connection between ballet and bubble gum? Because neurons that fire together wire together, we create certain mental models based on what's gone on in the past. If you hug your toddler every evening when you come home from work, he'll have a model in his mind that your return will be filled with affection and connection. This is because implicit memory creates something called "priming" in which the brain readies itself to respond in a certain way. When you get home, your son anticipates a hug. Not only is his internal world primed for receiving that loving gesture, he'll even move his arms in anticipation when he hears your car in the driveway. As he gets older, priming will continue to operate with more complex behaviors. A few years later, if a piano teacher frequently criticizes his playing, he may create a mental model that he doesn't like piano, or even that he's not musical. A more extreme version of this process occurs in the case of post-traumatic stress disorder, or PTSD, where an implicit memory of a disturbing experience becomes encoded in a person's brain, and a sound or image triggers that memory without the person even realizing it's a memory. Implicit memory is essentially an evolutionary process that keeps us safe and out of danger. It frees us to be able to react quickly, or even automate our responses in moments of danger without having to actively or intentionally recall previous similar experiences.

What all this means for us as parents is that when our kids seem to be reacting in unusually unreasonable ways, we need to consider whether an implicit memory has created a mental model that we need to help them explore. This is what Tina did for her son when she tucked him into bed and talked with him about the swimming lessons. Their conversation went something like this:

TINA: Can you tell me anything about what's going on with the swimming?

SON: I don't know, Mom. I just don't want to do it.

TINA: Are you afraid of something?

SON: I guess. I've just got all of these butterflies in my stomach.

TINA: So let's talk about those butterflies. Did you know that your brain remembers things even when you don't know you're remembering?

SON: I don't get it.

TINA: OK. Let me say it a different way. Do you remember you had a bad experience with swim lessons before?

SON: Oh yeah.

TINA: Do you remember that place we went?

SON: They were so hard on us there.

TINA: Those *were* some pretty strict teachers.

SON: They made me go off the diving board. And they dunked my head and made me hold my breath for a long time.

TINA: It was a long time, wasn't it? And you know what? I think that has a lot to do with why you don't want to go to swim lessons now.

SON: You do?

TINA: Yes. Do you know that lots of times when you do things, whether they are good or bad, your brain and body remember them? So when I say "Dodger Stadium" . . . You're smiling! Do you feel what's going on inside you now? What are your brain and body saying? How do you feel?

SON: Excited?

TINA: Yes. I can see that on your face. And do you feel butterflies in your stomach?

SON: No way.

TINA: And what about when I say "swimming lessons"?
Does that change how you feel?

SON: Uh-huh.

TINA: And the butterflies are back?

SON: Right. I don't want to go.

TINA: But here's what I think is going on. Your brain is amazing. And one of its important jobs is to keep you safe. See, your brain is always checking things out and saying, "This is good" or "This is bad." So when I say "Dodger Stadium," your brain says, "Good! Let's go! That's a fun place." But when I say "Swimming lessons," your brain says, "Bad idea. Don't go!"

SON: Exactly.

TINA: And the reason your brain gets so excited when I say "Dodger Stadium" is because you've had good experiences there. You probably don't remember every detail of every game, but still, you just have a good overall feeling about it.

You can see how Tina introduced this issue, just setting up the concept that certain memories can affect us without our awareness that something is coming from the past. You can also probably see why her son was nervous about swimming lessons. And one of the biggest problems was that he had no idea *why* he was nervous. He knew only that he didn't want to go. But when Tina explained where his feelings were coming from, he began to develop some awareness that let him take control over what was happening in his brain, so he could begin to reframe his experiences and his feelings.

They talked some more, then Tina introduced him to some practical tools he could use when he started feeling nervous about swimming lessons—some of the very tools we'll discuss with you in a few pages. Here's how the end of the conversation went.

TINA: OK, so now you know that the reason for your fear is that you had bad experiences before.

SON: Yeah, I guess.

TINA: But you're older and wiser now, and you can think

about swimming in whole new ways. So let's do a couple of things to help you feel better. One is to start thinking about all the memories you have of swimming that have been really fun and good. Can you think of a good swimming experience?

SON: Sure, when I was swimming with Henry last week.

TINA: Right. Good. And you can also talk to your brain.

SON: Huh?

TINA: Seriously. In fact, this is one of the best things you can do. You can say, "Brain, thanks for trying to keep me safe and protect me, but I don't need to be afraid of swimming anymore. These are new lessons with a new teacher, a new pool, and I'm a new kid who already knows how to swim. So, brain, I'm just going to blow out the butterflies from my stomach with some big, slow breaths, like this. And I'm going to focus on the good stuff about swimming." Does that seem weird, to talk to your brain like that?

SON: Kind of.

TINA: I know, it's funny and kind of strange. But do you see how it could work? What's something you could tell your brain to make your body calm down and make you feel safer and feel good about going to swimming lessons? What could you say in your mind?

SON: Those bad swimming lessons were just in the past. Now this is a new swim lesson, and I already like swimming.

TINA: Exactly. Because how do you feel about swimming in general?

SON: Great.

TINA: Great. And now let's do one more thing. What's something you could do or say to your brain if you start feeling nervous again when we first get to swimming lessons? Like a code to help remind yourself that these feelings are from the past?

SON: I don't know. Kill the butterflies?

TINA: Because the butterflies are from a long time ago and you don't need them in your stomach anymore, right?

SON: Right.

TINA: I love it. And I'm glad you're laughing about it now. But could we come up with a less violent code? How about "Liberate the butterflies" or "Free the butterflies"?

SON: I kind of like "kill."

TINA: OK. "Kill the butterflies" it is.

Notice that the main thing Tina did here was to tell the story of where her son's fears came from. She used narrative to help his implicit memories become explicit and full of meaning, so they wouldn't act on him with such hidden power. Once his implicit memories about the unpleasant swimming lessons were brought into the light of awareness, he could pretty easily deal with his present-day fears. It's in this transformation—from implicit to explicit—that the real power of integrating memory brings insight, understanding, and even healing.

INTEGRATING IMPLICIT AND EXPLICIT: ASSEMBLING THE PUZZLE PIECES OF THE MIND

Implicit memories are often positive and work in our favor, like when we fully expect to be loved by those around us simply because we've always been loved. If we count on our parents to comfort us when we're hurting, since they've always done so before, that's because a host of positive implicit memories have been stored up within us. But implicit memories can be negative as well, like when we've repeatedly had the opposite experience of our parents being irritated by or uninterested in our times of distress.

The problem with an implicit memory, especially of a painful or negative experience, is that when we aren't aware of it, it becomes a buried land mine that can limit us in significant and sometimes debilitating ways. The brain remembers many events whether we're aware of them or not, so when we have difficult experiences—anything from a twisted ankle to the death of someone we love—these painful moments get embedded in the brain and begin to affect us. Even though we're not aware of their origins in the past, implicit memories can still create fear, avoidance, sadness, and other painful emotions and bodily sensations. That helps explain why children (as well as adults) often react strongly to situations without being aware of why they are so upset. Unless kids can make sense of their painful memories, they may experience sleep disturbances, debilitating phobias, and other problems.

So how do we help our children when they're suffering from the effects of past negative experiences? We shine the light of awareness on those implicit memories, making them explicit so that our child can become aware of them and deal with them in an intentional way. Sometimes parents hope that their children will "just forget about" painful experiences they've undergone, but what kids really need is for parents to teach them healthy ways to integrate implicit and explicit memories, turning even painful experiences into sources of power and self-understanding.

There's a part of our brain whose very job is to do just that: to integrate our implicit and explicit memories, so that we can more fully understand the world and ourselves. It's called the hippocampus, and it can be considered the "search engine" of memory retrieval. The hippocampus works with different parts of our brain to take all of the images, emotions, and sensations of implicit memory and draw them together so that they can become the assembled "pictures" that make up our explicit understanding of our past experiences.

Think of the hippocampus as a master puzzle assembler that links together the jigsaw pieces of implicit memory. When the images and sensations of experience remain in implicit-only form, when they haven't been integrated by the hippocampus, they exist in isolation from one another as a jumbled mess in our brain. Instead of having a clear and whole picture, a completed jigsaw puzzle, our implicit memories remain scattered puzzle pieces. We therefore lack clarity about our own unfolding narrative, which explicitly defines who we are. What's worse, these implicit-only memories continue to shape the way we look at and interact with our here-and-now reality. They affect the sense of who we are from moment to moment—*all without our even being aware that they are affecting the way we interact with our world.*

It's crucial, therefore, that we assemble these implicit puzzle pieces into explicit form in order to be able to reflect on their impact on our lives. That's where the hippocampus comes in. By performing the important function of integrating implicit and explicit memories, it allows us to become the active authors of our own life stories. When Tina talked to her son about his fearful associations with swim lessons, she was simply helping his hippocampus do its job. It didn't take much for his implicit memories to become explicit, so that he could handle his fear and make sense of both his painful experience in the past and how it was still affecting him in the present.

When we don't offer a place for children to express their feelings and recall what happened after an overwhelming event, their implicit-only memories remain in dis-integrated form, leaving the children with no way to make sense of their experience. But when we help our kids integrate their past into their present, they can then make sense of what's going on inside them and gain control over how they think and behave. The more you promote this type of memory integration in your child, the less often you will see irrational responses to what's happening now that are really leftover reactions from the past.

We're not saying that memory integration is a parental cure-all that will prevent all outbursts and irrational reactions. But it is a powerful tool for dealing with difficult experiences from the past, and you'll be grateful to know about it the next time your child is struggling for some unknown reason. Granted, when your five-year-old can't find the taillight to complete Luke Skywalker's land cruiser and launches into an out-of-control yelling fit about "the stupid Lego store," that may have nothing to do with some sort of George Lucas–inspired implicit memory. In fact, before you overanalyze the situation, HALT and check the basics: is your little Jedi simply **h**ungry, **a**ngry, **l**onely, or **t**ired? If so, these problems can be fixed pretty easily. Get him an apple. Listen to his feelings of frustration. Spend a few minutes being with him, helping him locate the missing piece. Put him to bed earlier so he can catch up on his rest and handle himself better tomorrow. Often kids are doing their best; they just need us to attend to their basic needs. As you learn about the brain and consider all of the information we're offering here, don't forget about the simple and the obvious, the little things you already know. Common sense can take you a long way.

If, though, you determine that something bigger is going on, then it's a good idea to think back to experiences in the past that might be affecting the present situation. You may not always be able to tie your child's reactivity to a specific event in the past, so don't force a connection that's not there. But if you feel that a previous event may be influencing your child's actions, here are some practical ways you can arm him with tools that will help integrate his implicit and explicit memories and achieve more control in the way he responds to his present circumstances.

What You Can Do:
Helping Your Child Integrate Implicit and Explicit Memories

Whole-Brain Strategy #6:
Use the Remote of the Mind: Replaying Memories

Once again, one of the most effective ways to promote integration is to tell stories. In chapter 2, we talked about the importance of narrative in integrating the left and right hemispheres. Storytelling is also a powerful activity for integrating implicit and explicit memories. But sometimes, if a child is feeling the effects of an especially painful experience from the past, she may not be ready to remember the entire experience. In that case, you can introduce her to her internal DVD player, which comes with a remote control that lets her replay an experience in her mind. It can also pause, rewind, and fast-forward. Just like you might fast-forward through the scary parts of a movie or rewind to watch your favorite scene again, the remote of the mind is a tool that gives your child some control while revisiting an unpleasant memory. Here's how one father used this technique.

David's ten-year-old son, Eli, surprised him by saying that he didn't want to race a Pinewood Derby car this year with his Cub Scout troop. David was taken aback, because one of Eli's highlights every winter was working alongside his dad as they carved, shaped, and painted a block of pinewood until it was transformed into a sports car. After several conversations, David realized that Eli was unwilling to go anywhere near the woodworking tools, especially the ones with blades. From there it was fairly easy to make the connection between Eli's new phobia and an episode from months earlier.

The previous summer, Eli had taken his pocketknife to the park without his parents' permission. He and his friend Ryan had enjoyed cutting and whittling with the knife, until an accident occurred. While cutting a root, Ryan had sliced through it and jabbed the knife into his leg, leading to lots of blood and an ambulance ride to the emergency room. A few stitches later he was fine and didn't even seem too traumatized by the whole event. But Eli was beyond distressed as he waited at his house, wondering whether Ryan was OK. A compassionate, responsible boy, Eli couldn't get over the fact that it was his knife, taken to the park without permission, that had hurt his friend and caused so much trouble. The parents of the two boys got them together that evening and let them talk through what had happened, and both apparently moved on. But now, months later, the memory was clearly working on Eli again, without his knowledge. He apparently had no awareness that he was afraid of the woodworking tools because of what had happened with Ryan and the knife.

David decided to help Eli take that implicit memory and make it explicit. He called his son out to the garage, where he had his tools set up. As soon as Eli entered the garage and looked at the electric saw, his eyes widened and his dad saw fear on his face. He tried to appear normal as he said, "Dad, I don't want to do the Pinewood Derby this year."

David responded in his most nurturing voice. "I know, son, and I also think I know why."

He talked to Eli about the connection between the car race and the knife accident, but Eli resisted this explanation. He said, "No, that's not it. I'm just too busy with school right now."

But David pressed him. "I know you're busy, but I think there's more to it than that. Let's just talk again about what happened that day at the park."

Eli's face again showed fear. "Dad, that was a long time ago. We don't have to talk about it."

David reassured him, then he taught him a powerful technique for dealing with painful memories. He told his son, "I'm going to talk through the story, just the way you told it to me last summer. And I want you to imagine the story in your head, as if you were watching a DVD inside your brain."

Eli interrupted, "Dad, I *really* don't want to."

"I know you don't," David said. "But this is where the good part comes in. I want you to imagine that you're holding a remote control, just like the one we use when we watch movies in the house. And when I get to a part of the story you don't want to think about, you just hit pause. When you say 'Pause,' I'll stop. Then we can fast-forward past that scene. Can we do that?"

Eli said slowly, "OK"—the way kids do when they're responding to a request they think is crazy.

David proceeded to tell the story. He told about Eli's arrival at the park, about cutting bark with Ryan, and so on. When he said, "Then Ryan picked up a root and started to cut it," Eli broke in.

"Pause." He said it quietly, but with plenty of force.

David said, "OK. Now let's fast-forward to the hospital."

"Farther."

"To Ryan coming home?"

"Farther."

"To when he came over to our house that evening?"

"OK."

David then narrated the happy reunion between the friends—how they had greeted each other, then disappeared to go play video games. David stressed that Ryan and his parents had emphasized that they weren't upset with Eli and that they viewed the whole episode as an accident.

David looked at his son. "So that's the story, right?"

"Yup."

"Except there's that piece we left out."

"I know."

"Let's rewind and go back to where we paused and look at what happened. And remember, we've already seen that the story has a happy ending."

"OK."

INSTEAD OF FAST-FORWARD AND FORGET...

...TRY REWIND AND REMEMBER

David took Eli through the more painful parts of the narrative, and at times Eli used his pause button again. Eventually they made it through the story, and in doing so, Eli began to release his fears associated with knives and cutting. By the time they returned to the happy ending, David could see Eli's muscles relax, and the tension in his voice had dramatically decreased. Over the coming weeks they had to return to the story and retell it, and Eli still felt somewhat nervous around knives, but with the help of his father, Eli's hippocampus integrated his implicit memories into his explicit awareness. As a result, Eli could now deal with the issues that had resurfaced. He and his dad then built one of their best Pinewood Derby cars ever—and named it Fear Factor, writing the name on each side of the car in scary, Halloween-style letters.

Remember, your goal is to help your kids take the troubling experiences that are impacting them without their knowledge— the scattered puzzle pieces in their mind—and make those experiences explicit so that the whole picture in the puzzle can be seen with clarity and meaning. By introducing them to the remote of the mind, which controls their internal DVD player, you make the storytelling process much less scary, because you offer them some control over what they deal with, so they can interact with it at their own pace. They can then look at an experience that scared (or angered or frustrated) them without having to immediately relive it scene for scene.

Whole-Brain Strategy #7:
Remember to Remember: Making Recollection a Part of Your Family's Daily Life

The act of remembering comes naturally for most people. But memory is like so many functions of the brain: the more we exercise it, the stronger it becomes. That means that when you give your children lots of practice at remembering—by having them tell and retell their own stories—you improve their ability to integrate implicit and explicit memories.

So our second suggestion is simply that you remember to remember. During your various activities, help your kids talk about their experiences, so they can integrate their implicit and explicit memories. This is especially important when it comes to the most important and valuable moments of their lives. The more you can help bring those noteworthy moments into their explicit memory—such as family experiences, important friendships, or rites of passage—then the clearer and more influential those experiences will be.

There are plenty of practical ways to encourage your kids to remember. The most natural is to ask questions that lead to recollection. With very young children, keep things simple, focusing on returning their attention to the details of their day. *Did you go to Carrie's house today? What happened when we got there?* Just recounting basic facts like this helps develop your child's memory and prepares her for interacting with more significant memories down the road.

As kids get older, you can be more strategic regarding what you focus on. Ask about a problem they had with a friend or teacher, a party they went to, or the details from last night's play rehearsal. Or encourage them to journal. Studies have clearly shown that the very act of recalling and expressing an event through journaling can improve immune and heart function, as well as general well-being. More to the point here, though, it gives kids a chance to tell their stories, which aids them in the meaning-making process that improves their ability to understand their past and present experiences.

When we speak to parents about memory integration and encourage them to help their kids talk about their experiences, one question inevitably comes up: *What if they won't talk?* Or *What if I ask about the art class, and all they say is, "It was OK"?* If you have trouble drawing out some meaty details about your child's life, be creative. One trick for younger school-age kids is to play a guessing game when you pick them up from school. Say, "Tell me two things that really happened today, and one thing that didn't. Then I'll guess which two are true." The game may lack a certain amount of challenge for you—especially when your choices include "Ms. Derrick read us a story," "Me and Nico spied on the girls," and "Captain Hook captured me and fed me to the alligator"—but it can quickly become a fun game that kids look forward

INSTEAD OF "HOW WAS YOUR DAY?"...

...TRY REMEMBER TO REMEMBER

to. It will not only open up their lives to you, since you get to hear about two of their memories from school each day, but it can also help them get used to thinking back and reflecting on the events of their days.

Another mom who had recently divorced wanted to make sure that she stayed emotionally connected to her daughters as they went through that difficult period. So she began the ritual of asking, as they ate dinner together each evening, "Tell me about your day. Give me one high point, one low point, and one act of kindness you performed for someone." Again, activities and questions like these not only encourage recollection but also push children to think more deeply about their own emotions and actions, about sharing their days with someone, and about how they can help others.

For specific events you want your child to think more about, look at photo albums and watch old videos. One great way to help them focus in more depth is to design and illustrate a "memory book" with your child. For example, when your daughter returns from her first sleepaway camp, you can collect the letters she sent home, pieces of memorabilia, and the photos she took, and create a memory book with her. She can write little stories and notes in the margins: "This was my cabin," or "This was after the shaving-cream fight." Creating a book like this prompts your daughter's memory about some of the details she might otherwise lose in the coming months and years, while also giving her the opportunity to share with you more about this important event in her life.

Simply by asking questions and encouraging recollection, you can help your kids remember and understand important events from the past, which will help them better understand what's happening to them in the present.

Whole-Brain Kids:
Teach Your Kids About Making Their Implicit Memories Explicit

We've given you several examples of how to talk to your kids about implicit and explicit memories. If you notice that your child is struggling as a result of a past experience, one of the best things you can do is to talk to him and help him retell the story of that experience. But it can also be helpful to explain what's happening in the brain when a past experience begins to control present behaviors and feelings. You might explain it like this:

PUTTING PUZZLE PIECES OF MEMORY TOGETHER

WHEN THINGS HAPPEN, YOUR BRAIN REMEMBERS THEM, BUT NOT ALWAYS AS A WHOLE, PUT-TOGETHER MEMORY. INSTEAD, IT'S AS IF THERE ARE LITTLE PUZZLE PIECES OF WHAT HAPPENED FLOATING AROUND IN YOUR HEAD.

THE WAY YOU HELP YOUR BRAIN PUT THE PUZZLE PIECES TOGETHER IS BY TELLING THE STORY OF WHAT HAPPENED.

TELLING THE STORY IS GREAT WHEN WE DO SOMETHING FUN, LIKE HAVING A BIRTHDAY PARTY. JUST BY TALKING ABOUT IT, WE GET TO REMEMBER HOW MUCH FUN WE HAD.

BUT SOMETIMES, SOMETHING UPSETTING HAPPENS TO US, AND WE MIGHT NOT WANT TO RE-MEMBER. THE PROBLEM IS THAT WHEN WE DON'T THINK ABOUT IT THOSE PUZZLE PIECES NEVER GET PUT TOGETHER, AND WE MIGHT FEEL SCARED, SAD, OR ANGRY WITHOUT KNOWING WHY.

FOR EXAMPLE:

THIS IS WHAT HAPPENED TO MIA. SHE DIDN'T KNOW WHY SHE WAS SCARED OF DOGS. THEN ONE DAY HER DAD TOLD HER A STORY SHE'D FORGOTTEN ABOUT THE TIME A BIG DOG HAD BARKED AT HER.

SHE SAW THAT HER FEARS WERE ABOUT THAT TIME AND NOT ABOUT DOGS SHE MEETS NOW.

NOW SHE LIKES TO PET FRIENDLY DOGS IN HER NEIGHBORHOOD, AND SHE EVENS WANTS A PUPPY OF HER OWN.

WHEN YOU TELL THE STORY ABOUT WHAT HAPPENED, YOU PUT THE PUZZLE PIECES TOGETHER AND YOU FEEL LESS SCARED, SAD, OR ANGRY. YOU WILL ALSO FEEL BRAVER, CALMER, AND HAPPIER.

Integrating Ourselves: Moving Our Own Memories from Implicit to Explicit

Kids aren't the only ones whose memories can intrude on their lives when they don't even know it. It happens, of course, to parents as well. Implicit memories influence our behaviors, emotions, perceptions, and even physical sensations, and we can remain completely ignorant of the past's influence on us in the present moment. Dan experienced this firsthand as a new parent:

When my son was first born I would come unglued when he cried inconsolably. I know a baby's cry is hard for anyone to hear, but I just couldn't take it. Panic would set in, and I'd become filled with dread and terror. I explored theory after theory for my intense and seemingly unwarranted reaction, but none of them rang true.

Then one day my son began to cry and an image came to my mind. It was a small boy on an examining table, screaming, with a look of terror on his scrunched-up, reddened face. I was next to him, and my job, as a young pediatric intern at the UCLA Medical Center, was to draw blood from him so we could figure out why he had such a high fever. My pediatric partner and I had to relive this horror with child after child, one of us holding the syringe, the other holding down the screaming child.

I hadn't thought about my pediatrics internship in years. I remembered it as a good year overall, and I recalled being glad when it was over. But the middle-of-the-night cries of my six-month-old son triggered my flashback to this scene, and over the days that followed, I began to understand the connection. I thought a lot about those memories and talked to a few friends and colleagues about my experience. It began to be clear to me that this trauma from years earlier had remained implicit and was surfacing explicitly only now. I realized that I had completed my yearlong internship and moved on to the next phase of my life, never having consciously reflected on my painful experiences. I never processed them in a way that would make them readily available for later explicit retrieval.

Years later, then, as a young parent, I went through the painful self-reflection that allowed me to see this as an unresolved issue in myself, and I was able to hear my son's cries for what they were, without all the baggage from the past.

Unexamined (or dis-integrated) memories cause all kinds of problems for any adult trying to live a healthy, relational life. But for parents, these hidden memories are especially dangerous, for two main reasons. First of all, even when they're very young, our kids can pick up on our feelings of dread or distress or inadequacy, even if we don't realize we're experiencing them. And when a parent is upset, it's very difficult for a child to remain calm and happy. Second, implicit memories can trigger responses from us that cause us to act in ways we don't want to. Old feelings of being left out, abandoned, or put down, by others or by our own parents, can keep us from being mature, loving, and respectful when we interact with our kids.

So the next time you find yourself reacting a bit too strongly when you're upset with your kids, ask yourself, "Is my response here making sense?"

The answer may be, "Yes. The baby's screaming, my three-year-old just painted the oven blue, and all my eight-year-old is doing in response is turning up the TV. It makes perfect sense that I feel like throwing something through the window!"

At other times, though, the answer may be, "No, these feelings don't make sense. There's no reason for me to take it personally that my daughter wants Daddy to read to her tonight instead of me. I don't need to be this upset." Based on what you now know about implicit memory, an insight like this is an opportunity to look deeper. If you're reacting in ways you can't explain or justify, it's probably time to ask, "What's going on here? Is this reminding me of something? And where in the world are my feelings and behavior coming from?" (We'll talk more about this process in the "Integrating Ourselves" section of chapter 6. Also, we recommend Dan's book *Parenting from the Inside Out,* written with Mary Hartzell, as a great place to begin this journey of exploration.)

By integrating your implicit and explicit memories and shining the light of awareness on difficult moments from your past, you can gain insight into how your past is impacting your relationship with your children. You can remain watchful for how your issues are affecting your own mood as well as how your kids feel. When you feel incompetent, frustrated, or overly reactive, you can look at what's behind those feelings and explore whether they are connected to something in your past. Then you can bring your former experiences into the present and weave them into the larger story of your life. When you do that, you can be free to be the kind of parent you want to be. You can make sense of your own life, which will help your kids do the same with theirs.

CHAPTER 5

The United States of Me

Integrating the Many Parts of the Self

"Is there anything Josh *can't* do?"

This was the question other parents asked Amber about her bright and talented eleven-year-old. Josh seemed to excel at everything—school, sports, music, and social activities—and his friends and their parents marveled at his abilities.

Amber, however, knew that no matter how much success he achieved, Josh struggled with serious doubts about his own self-worth. As a result, he felt an overpowering need to be perfect at everything he attempted. This perfectionism left him believing that, despite his many successes, nothing he did was good enough. He beat himself up emotionally whenever he made a mistake, whether it was missing a shot in a basketball game or forgetting his lunch box at school.

Eventually Amber took Josh to see Tina, who soon learned that his parents had divorced when he was an infant and his father had disappeared, leaving him to be raised by his mother. Over time, it became apparent that Josh blamed himself for his father's absence, believing that he had somehow caused his dad to leave, and now he did everything within his power to avoid making mistakes of any kind. Josh's implicit memory had equated not being perfect with abandonment. As a result, the thoughts running through his head on a daily basis—"I should've done better"; "I'm so stupid"; "Why did I do that?"—were keeping him from being a happy, carefree eleven-year-old.

Tina began working with Josh on paying attention to those thoughts in his mind. Some were fueled by deeply embedded implicit memories that required an in-depth approach for healing. But she also helped him understand the power of his mind, and how by directing his attention, he could take control and, to a great extent, actually *choose* how he felt, and how he wanted to respond to different situations. For Josh, the breakthrough came when Tina introduced him to the idea of mindsight.

MINDSIGHT AND THE WHEEL OF AWARENESS

Dan coined the term "mindsight," and as he explains in his book of the same name, the simplest meaning of the word comes down to two things: understanding our own mind as well as understanding the mind of another. Connecting with others will be the focus of the next chapter. For now, though, let's focus on the first aspect of the mindsight approach, understanding our own mind. After all, that's where mental health and well-being begin, with achieving clarity and insight into our own individual mind. That's the idea Tina began teaching Josh about. She introduced him to a model that Dan created, the wheel of awareness.

The basic concept, as you can see from the diagram on page 94, is that our mind can be pictured as a bicycle wheel, with a hub at the center and spokes radiating toward the outer rim. The rim represents anything we can pay attention to or become aware of: our thoughts and feelings, our dreams and desires, our memories, our perceptions of the outside world, and the sensations from our body.

The hub is the inner place of the mind from which we become aware of all that's happening around and within us. It's basically our prefrontal cortex, which you'll remember helps to integrate the whole brain. The hub represents part of what's called the executive brain, because it's from this place that we make our best

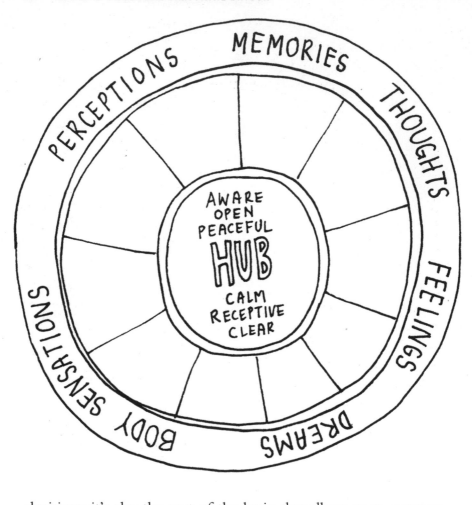

decisions; it's also the part of the brain that allows us to connect deeply to others and to ourselves. Our awareness resides in the hub, and from here we can focus on the various points on the rim of our wheel.

The wheel-of-awareness model was immediately powerful for Josh since it allowed him to recognize that the different thoughts and feelings giving him so much trouble were simply different *aspects* of himself. They were just a few particular rim points on his wheel, and he didn't have to give them so much attention. (See the diagram of Josh's personal wheel of awareness on page 95.) Tina helped him see that each set of rim points he focused on determined his state of mind at any given moment. In other words, his anxious and fearful state of mind came about because he was

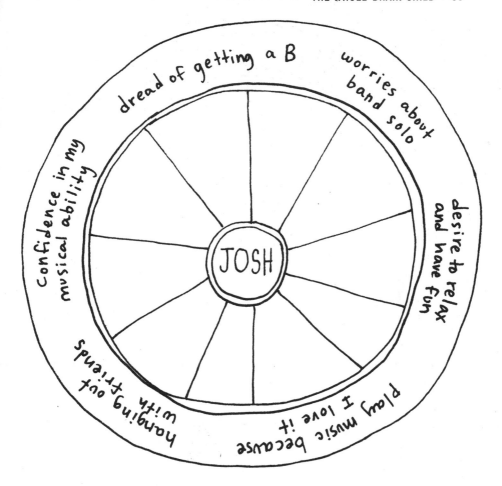

focusing on a set of anxiety-producing rim points—like his dread of receiving a B on his homework, or his worries about forgetting the notes during his band solo. Even the physical sensations he experienced, the anxious knot in his stomach and the tension in his shoulders, were rim points that kept him focused on his fear of failure.

Mindsight let him see what was happening in his own mind, so he could understand that *he* was the one giving all this time and energy to these rim points, and that if he wanted, he could return to his hub, where he could see the big picture and focus on other rim points instead. Those fears and worries were definitely part of him, but they didn't represent the totality of his being. Instead, from his hub at the center of the wheel, which was the most thoughtful and objective part of himself, he could *choose* how much attention to give them, as well as which other rim points he wanted to focus on.

As Tina explained to him, in giving all of his attention to these few fearful rim points, Josh was excluding many other rim points he could integrate into his perspective on the world. That left him spending all of his time working and studying and practicing and worrying, when he could have been paying attention to other, more productive rim points, like his confidence in his musical ability, his belief that he was smart, and his desire to just relax and have fun from time to time. Tina explained to Josh the importance of integrating the different parts of himself, the unique aspects of who he is, so that a few of them didn't completely dominate all of the others. It was fine, she told him, to pay attention to the rim points that pushed him to achieve and excel. These were good and even healthy parts of himself. But those points needed to be integrated with the others so that he didn't forsake the other parts of himself, which were also good and healthy.

So Josh started working on directing his focus toward points that didn't necessarily lead to perfectionism. He began paying special attention to the part of himself that loves just hanging out with his friends after school, even if that meant giving up some study time. He focused on his newly formed belief that he didn't have to be the leading scorer in every game. And he used his self-talk to remind himself how good he feels when he plays his saxophone just for pleasure, not worrying about hitting every note perfectly. He didn't have to stop wanting to achieve and succeed. He just needed to put those rim points into context with the others, to integrate them so that they were just a few various parts of a much greater whole, a much bigger Josh than the one who would criticize himself for every little mistake.

Learning about mindsight and the wheel of awareness didn't, of course, immediately alleviate Josh's drive toward perfectionism. But it did help him begin to accept that he didn't have to stay miserable. He saw that he could make choices to improve difficult circumstances by making decisions that little by little allowed him to take control of how he experienced and responded to different situations. (He and Tina did have to laugh together, though, when he began to feel frustrated with himself when he wasn't perfect at worrying less about being perfect.)

STUCK ON THE RIM: DISTINGUISHING BETWEEN "FEEL" AND "AM"

Josh's suffering was a result of being "stuck on the rim" of the wheel of awareness. Rather than perceiving his world from his hub and integrating his many rim points, he directed all of his attention toward just a few particular rim points that created an anxious and critical state of mind. As a result, he lost touch with many of the other parts of the rim that could help him experience a more peaceful and accepting state of mind. This is what happens when kids aren't working from an integrated wheel of awareness. Just like adults, they can become stuck on certain rim points, on one or a few particular aspects of their being, which often leads to experiencing rigidity or chaos.

This leaves them confusing the difference between "feel" and "am." When children experience a particular state of mind, such as feeling frustrated or lonely, they may be tempted to define themselves based on that temporary experience, as opposed to understanding that that's simply how they feel *at the moment*. Instead of saying, "I *feel* lonely" or "I *feel* sad right now," they say, "I *am* lonely" or "I *am* sad." The danger is that the temporary state of mind can be perceived as a permanent part of their self. The *state* comes to be seen as a *trait* that defines who they are.

Imagine, for instance, a nine-year-old who is struggling with her homework, even though school usually comes fairly easily to her. Unless she integrates her feelings of frustration and inadequacy with the other parts of herself—realizing that one emotion is just a part of a larger whole of who she is—she might begin to look at this momentary state as a more permanent trait or characteristic of her personality. She might say something like, "I'm so stupid. Homework is too hard for me. I'll never get it right."

But if her parents can help her integrate the many parts of herself, recognizing the various rim points on her wheel, she can avoid identifying solely with this one particular feeling in this one particular moment. She can develop the mindsight to realize that she's frustrated about struggling in this moment, but it doesn't mean that she's dumb or that she'll always have trouble. From the hub of her mind, she can notice various rim points and realize that even though she's struggling at the moment, she has demonstrated in the past that she can usually handle homework without this much trouble. She might even use some healthy self-talk, saying to herself, "I hate this homework! It's driving me crazy! But I know I'm smart. It's just that this assignment is really hard." The simple act of acknowledging different points along the rim can take her a long way toward gaining control and shifting her negative feelings. She may still *feel* dumb, but with her parents' help and with some practice, she'll be able to avoid seeing that temporary state as a permanent, self-defining trait.

This is one of the best things the wheel of awareness does: it teaches kids that they have choices about what they focus on and where they place their attention. It gives them a tool that lets them integrate the different parts of themselves, so they aren't held hostage by one negative constellation of feelings or thoughts clamoring for their attention. When children (and adults, for that matter) can develop this type of mindsight, they become empowered to make choices that allow them to manage their experiences as well as how they respond to their world. Over time, with practice, they learn to direct their attention in ways that are most helpful to themselves and to those around them, even during difficult moments.

THE POWER OF FOCUSED ATTENTION

To understand why mindsight offers such empowering choices, it's helpful to understand what happens in the brain when a person concentrates on one particular set of rim points. As we've discussed already, the brain physically changes in response to new experiences. With intention and effort, we can acquire new mental skills. What's more, when we direct our attention in a new way, we are actually creating a new experience that can change both the activity and ultimately the structure of the brain itself.

Here's how it works. When we have a new experience or concentrate on something—say, on how we feel or a goal we'd like to achieve—that activates neural firing. In other words, neurons (our brain cells) spring into action. This neural firing leads to the production of proteins that enable new connections to be wired among the activated neurons. Remember, neurons that fire together wire together. This entire process—from neural activation to neural growth and strengthened connections—is *neuroplasticity*. Essentially, it means that the brain itself is plastic, or changing, based on what we experience, and what we give our attention to. And these new neural connections, created when we pay attention to something, in turn alter the way we respond to and interact with our world. This is how practice can become a skill and how a state can become a trait, for good or for bad.

There's a lot of scientific evidence demonstrating that focused attention leads to the reshaping of the brain. In animals rewarded for noticing sound (to hunt or to avoid being hunted, for example), we find much larger auditory centers in the brain. In animals rewarded for sharp eyesight, the visual areas are larger. Brain scans of violinists provide more evidence, showing dramatic growth and expansion in regions of the cortex that represent the left hand, which has to finger the strings precisely, often at very high speed. Other studies have shown that the hippocampus, which is vital for spatial memory, is enlarged in taxi drivers. The point is that the physical architecture of the brain changes according to where we direct our attention and what we practice doing.

We recently saw this principle at work in Jason, a six-year-old. At times Jason would obsess about irrational fears, and it was driving his parents crazy. Eventually he began having trouble sleeping because he was afraid the ceiling fan in his bedroom would come crashing down on him. His parents had repeatedly shown him how securely the fan was attached and logically explained how safe he was in his bed. But the thoughts from his rational, logical upstairs brain were being hijacked each night by the fears in his

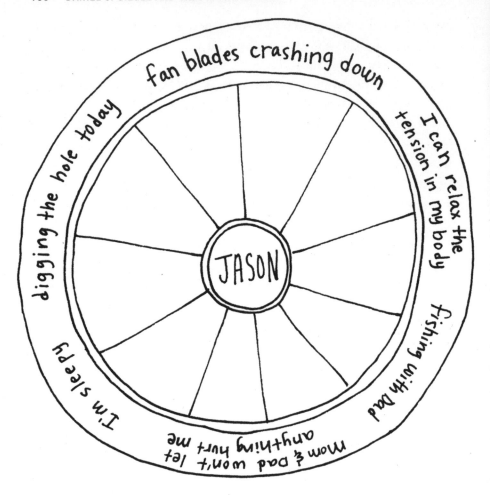

downstairs brain. He would lie awake long past bedtime worrying what would happen if the screws came loose and the twirling blades descended on him, chopping into pieces his body, his bed, and his Darth Vader sheets.

Once his parents learned about mindsight and explained the wheel of awareness to him, Jason suddenly had a valuable tool that offered relief not only to himself but also to his whole family. He saw that, like Josh, he had become stuck on his rim, fixating on his fear of what might happen if the ceiling fan fell. His parents helped him get back to his hub where he could recognize the physical sensations that signaled that this obsession was creeping into his mind—the anxious feelings in his chest, the tension in his arms, legs, and face—so he could then direct his attention toward something that would relax him. Then he could take the next steps to bring together the different parts of himself. He could think about other rim points: his confidence that his parents would protect him and would never let him sleep beneath a fan that might fall and hurt him, or his memory of how much fun he'd had that day digging the huge hole in the backyard. Or he could focus on the tension he felt in his body and use some guided imagery to help himself relax. Jason loves to fish, so he learned to picture himself in a boat with his father. (We'll say more about this technique in a minute.)

Again, it all comes back to awareness. By becoming aware that he was stuck on one part of the rim of his wheel, and realizing that he had other options regarding where he directed his concentration, Jason learned to shift his focus and therefore his mental state. That meant he could then make decisions that made life much easier for both himself and his family. They all survived this difficult phase without having to remove the ceiling fan.

But once again, integration led not only to surviving, but to thriving as well. Mindsight wasn't just a Band-Aid for Jason that helped him and his parents deal with one particular difficult nighttime obstacle. It also produced a more fundamental change that will create benefits long into adulthood. In other words, learning to use the wheel of awareness and change where his attention was directed naturally changed Jason's perspective—but it did much more than that. As Jason, even at such a young age, understood this principle and practiced concentrating on other rim points, the neurons in his brain fired in new ways and made new connections. These new firings and wirings changed the makeup of his brain and left him less vulnerable not only to this particular fear and this particular obsession, but to future fears and obsessions as well—like when he felt petrified about singing onstage for the holiday concert at his school, and nervous about going on a sleepover at his friend's house. Mindsight, along with the awareness it brought, actually changed Jason's brain. Because of his nature, he may continue to deal with certain worries that come with his personality. But for the rest of his life, he'll reap the benefit of this whole-brain work he's done as a young child, and he'll have at his disposal a powerful tool for dealing with other fears and obsessions.

As Jason's mother and father found out, mindsight can be a thrilling discovery for parents, especially when they see the power of integration at work in their child's life. It's very exciting to understand (and to teach our kids) that we can use our minds to take control of our lives. By directing our attention, we can go from *being influenced* by factors within and around us to *influencing* them. When we become aware of the multitude of changing emotions and forces at work around us and within us, we can acknowledge them and even embrace them as parts of ourselves—but we don't have to allow them to bully us or define us. We can shift our focus to other rim points on the wheel of awareness, so that we are no longer victims of forces seemingly beyond our control, but active participants in the process of deciding and affecting how we think and feel.

What an amazing power to bestow on your children! When they understand some basic mindsight principles—and kids can often get the wheel of awareness idea at a very young age, even at the beginning of elementary school—they are empowered to more fully regulate their own bodies and minds and actually change the way they experience different life situations. Their downstairs brain and implicit memories will control them less, and their mindsight will help them live full and healthy lives from an integrated brain.

But what if children get stuck on the rim and can't seem to get back to their hub? In other words, what if they can't seem to bring together the different parts of themselves because they are so fixated on one particular state of mind? As parents, we know that this "stuckness" happens all the time. Just think about Josh and his perfectionism. Even once he understands about the wheel of awareness and the different parts of himself, his need to excel may still overpower him at times. The same goes for Jason and his fear of the ceiling fan. An awareness of mindsight and the wheel of awareness can be very powerful, but that doesn't mean kids can easily switch the focus of their attention onto another rim point and move on with their lives.

So how can we help our kids increasingly integrate the different parts of themselves and become unstuck on rim points that are limiting them? How can we help them develop mindsight so they can more and more access its power to control their own lives? Let's talk about a few ways you can introduce mindsight to your kids and help them build skills they can use on a daily basis.

What You Can Do:
Introducing Your Child to the Power of Mindsight

Whole-Brain Strategy #8:
Let the Clouds of Emotions Roll By: Teaching That Feelings Come and Go

As we've said repeatedly in our journey through this book, it's very important that kids learn about and understand their feelings. But it's also true that feelings need to be recognized for what they are: temporary, changing conditions. They are states, not traits. They're like the weather. Rain is real, and we'd be foolish to stand in a downpour and act as if it weren't actually raining. But we'd be just as foolish to expect that the sun will never reappear.

We need to help children understand that the clouds of their emotions can (and will) roll on by. They won't feel sad or angry or hurt or lonely forever. This is a difficult concept for kids to understand at first. When they hurt or when they're scared, it's sometimes hard for them to imagine that they won't *always* suffer. Taking the long view isn't usually that easy even for an adult, much less a young child.

So we have to help them understand that feelings are temporary—on average, an emotion comes and goes in ninety seconds. If we can communicate to our children how fleeting most feelings are, then we can help them develop the mindsight on display in the boy we mentioned earlier who corrected himself and said, "I'm not dumb; I just *feel* dumb right now."

Younger kids will obviously need your help, but they can certainly grasp the idea that feelings come and go. The more kids understand that feelings come and go, the less they'll get stuck on the rim of their wheel, and the more they'll be able to live life and make decisions from their hub.

INSTEAD OF DISMISS AND DENY...

...TRY TEACHING THAT FEELINGS COME AND GO

Whole-Brain Strategy #9:
SIFT: Paying Attention to What's Going On Inside

In order for kids to develop mindsight and then influence the different thoughts, desires, and emotions whirling around within them, they first need to become aware of what it is they are actually experiencing. That means one of our most important parenting jobs is to help our children recognize and understand the different rim points of their individual wheel of awareness.

You don't have to have a serious sit-down meeting to communicate this idea. Find ways to work with the concept during your daily interactions with your kids. Tina recently decided the idea would be helpful in changing her seven-year-old son's mood as she was driving him to school one morning. He was upset that his trip to Dodger Stadium had been postponed, so she took the opportunity to introduce him to the "windshield of awareness": "Look at all the spots on our windshield. These spots are like all the different things you are thinking and feeling right now. There are a lot! See this smudge right here? That's how mad you feel at Dad right now. And those yellow bug guts? That's your disappointment that you're not going to get to go to the game tonight. But see that splat right there? That's how much you believe Dad when he says he'll take you next weekend. And that one there is how you know you can have a good day today anyway because you get to eat lunch and play kickball at recess with Ryan. . . ." You can use anything available to you: a windshield, an actual bicycle wheel, a piano keyboard, or whatever is nearby. Just help your kids understand that there are many parts of themselves that they can get to know and integrate with one another.

One of the best ways to begin orienting kids to what's on their rim is to help them learn to SIFT through all the **s**ensations, **i**mages, **f**eelings, and **t**houghts that are affecting them. By paying attention to their physical *sensations*, for example, children can become much more aware of what's going on inside their bodies. They can learn to recognize stomach butterflies as markers of anxiety, a desire to hit as anger or frustration, heavy shoulders as sadness, and so on. They can identify tension in their body when they're nervous, then learn to relax their shoulders and take deep breaths to calm themselves. Simply recognizing different sensations like hunger, tiredness, excitement, and grumpiness can give children a great deal of understanding and ultimately influence over their feelings.

In addition to sensations, we need to teach our kids to SIFT for *images* that are affecting the way they look at and interact with the world. Some images remain from the past, like the memory of a parent on a hospital gurney, or an embarrassing moment at school. Others might be fabricated from their imaginations or even nightmares they've had. A child who worries about being left out and isolated at recess might, for example, picture herself on a lonely swing by herself. Or another child might struggle with nighttime fears as a result of the images he remembers from a scary dream. When a child becomes aware of the images that are active in his mind, he can use his mindsight to take control of those images and greatly diminish the power they have over him.

Kids can also be taught to SIFT for *feelings* and emotions they are experiencing. Take time to ask kids how they feel, and help them be specific, so they can go from vague emotional descriptors like "fine" and "bad" to more precise ones, like "disappointed," "anxious," "jealous," and "excited." One reason kids often don't express the complexity of a particular emotion is that they haven't yet learned to think about their feelings in a sophisticated way that recognizes the variety and richness within them. As a result, they don't use a full spectrum of emotions in their responses, and instead paint their emotional pictures primarily in black and white. Ideally, we want our kids to recognize that there's a colorful rainbow of rich emotions within them, and to pay attention to these different possibilities.

Without mindsight into what's going on in their whole brain, they'll be trapped in black and white, like old TV reruns we watch over and over again. When they have a full emotional palette, they are able to experience the vivid Technicolor that a deep and vibrant emotional life allows. This teaching takes place, again, in your everyday interactions with your kids, and it begins before they can even talk. *I know it's disappointing that you can't have the*

INSTEAD OF DISMISS AND DENY...

...TRY USING MINDSIGHT TO TAKE CONTROL OF IMAGES

FEELINGS

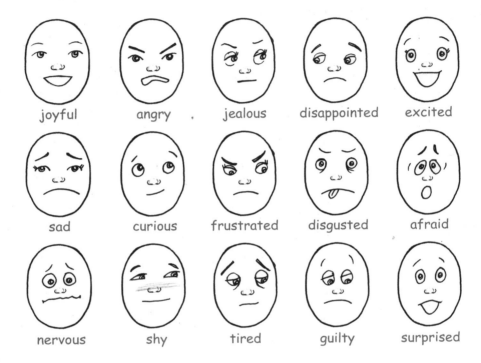

candy. Then as they get older you can increasingly introduce them to more subtleties of emotion. *I'm sorry your ski trip got canceled. If that happened to me, I'd be feeling all kinds of things: mad, disappointed, hurt, let down. What else?*

Thoughts are different from feelings, sensations, and images in that they represent the more left-brained part of the SIFTing process. They are what we think about, what we tell ourselves, and how we narrate the story of our own lives, using words. Kids can learn to pay attention to the thoughts running through their heads, and understand that they don't have to believe every one of them.

They can even argue with the ideas that aren't helpful or healthy—or even true. Through this self-talk they can direct their attention away from rim points that are limiting them, and toward those that lead to happiness and growth. Mindsight lets them return to their hub and pay attention to their thoughts. Then, from that place of awareness, they can use self-talk to remind themselves of other rim points, of other thoughts and feelings that are also important parts of themselves. For example, an eleven-year-old girl might look in the mirror and say, "So stupid to get sunburned at camp. So stupid!" But if her parents have taught her to argue with her own negative thoughts, she might take a step back and correct herself: "Come on, that's not stupid. It's normal to forget things sometimes. Almost all the kids got too much sun today."

By teaching our children to SIFT through the activity of their mind, we can help them recognize the different rim points at work within them, and help them gain more insight and control in their lives. Notice, too, how integrated the whole process is when it comes to how the brain takes in different stimuli. The nervous system extends throughout our body, functioning like powerful antennae that read the different physical sensations from our five senses. Then we draw on the images from the right hemisphere of the brain, combining these with the feelings that arise from the right brain and the limbic system. Then ultimately we link everything together with the conscious thoughts that originate in our left hemisphere and the analytical skills from our upstairs brain. SIFTing helps us understand the important lesson that our bodily sensations shape our emotion and our emotion shapes our thinking, as well as the images in our mind. The influences go the other way, too: if we are thinking hostile thoughts, we can increase a feeling of anger that in turn can make our body's muscles tense up. All of the points on the rim—sensations, images, feelings, and thoughts—can influence the others, and together they create our state of mind.

The next time you have a few minutes in the car with your kids, play the SIFT game, asking questions that aid the SIFTing process. Here's an example of how you can begin:

YOU:	I'll mention something about what the sensations of my body are telling me. I'm hungry. What about you? What's your body saying?
YOUR CHILD:	The seat belt feels scratchy on my neck.
YOU:	Oh, that's a good one. I'll adjust it in a minute. What about images? What pictures are going through your mind? I'm remembering that hilarious scene from your school play, and you in that funny hat.
YOUR CHILD:	I'm thinking about the preview we saw for that new movie. The one about the aliens?
YOU:	Yeah, we've got to see that. Now feelings. I'm really feeling excited about Grandma and Grandpa coming tomorrow.
YOUR CHILD:	Me, too!
YOU:	OK, S-I-F . . . Now *T* for "thoughts." I just thought about how we need milk. We'll need to stop before we get home. What about you?
YOUR CHILD:	I've been thinking that Claire should have to do more chores than me, since she's older.
YOU:	(smiling) I'm glad you're so good at coming up with ideas. We'll have to give that one some more thought.

Even if things get silly, the SIFT game is a good way to give your kids practice at paying attention to their inner landscape. And remember that just by talking about the mind, you help develop it.

Whole-Brain Strategy #10:
Exercise Mindsight: Getting Back to the Hub

We've talked above about the power of mindsight and focused attention. When kids become fixated on one set of points on their wheel of awareness, we need to help them shift their focus so that they can become more integrated. They can then see that they don't have to be victims of the sensations, images, feelings, and thoughts within them, and *decide* how they think and feel about their experiences.

This doesn't come naturally to children, but they can readily be taught how to focus their attention back to the hub. We can give them tools and strategies for calming themselves and integrating their different feelings and desires. One of the best ways parents can do this is to introduce them to mindsight exercises that help them get back to the hub. When we help our children return to the hub of their wheel, we help them become more focused and centered so they can remain aware of the many rim points affecting their emotions and state of mind.

Here's how one mother, Andrea, helped her nine-year-old, Nicole, get back to her hub so she could deal with her anxiety about an upcoming music recital. On the morning of the recital, Andrea realized that Nicole was understandably nervous about playing her violin in front of her friends and their parents. She knew her daughter's feelings were normal, but she also wanted to help her become less stuck on her rim. So she introduced her to a mindsight exercise. Andrea had Nicole lie flat on the sofa, and she sat in the chair next to her. Then she began to help her daughter become more aware of what was going on inside her. Here's the gist of what she said:

OK, Nicole, while you're lying still, move your eyes around the room. Even without moving your head, you can see the lamp over on the table. Now look over at your baby pictures. See them? Now look at the bookcase. Can you see the big Harry Potter book there? Now look back at the lamp.

Do you see how you have the power to focus your attention all over this room? That's what I want to teach you about, but we're going to focus your attention on what's going on inside your mind and body. Close your eyes, and let's focus on your thoughts and feelings and senses. Let's start with what you hear. I'm going to be quiet for a few seconds, and you pay attention to the sounds around us.

What do you hear? That car going by? The dog barking across the street? Do you hear your brother running the water in the bathroom? You're aware of those sounds simply because you got still and focused on hearing them. You listened on purpose.

Now I want you to notice your breathing. First, notice the

air coming in and out of your nose. . . . Now feel your chest going up and down. . . . Now notice the way your stomach moves each time you breathe in and out. . . .

I'm going to be quiet again for a few seconds. During that time, stay focused on your breath. Other thoughts will come into your mind, and you'll probably even think about the recital. That's fine. When you notice that your mind is wandering and you're thinking about something else or starting to worry, just go back to focusing on your breath. Follow that wave of the in-breath and the out-breath.

After a minute or so Andrea had Nicole open her eyes and sit up. Andrea explained that this technique is a powerful way to calm the mind and body. She told her to keep this exercise in her pocket for when she needed it—for instance, just before the recital. If she began to feel her heart pounding just before she played her violin, she could return to thinking about her breath coming in and going out, even with her eyes open.

You can see how a calming mindsight exercise like this could be a simple but powerful tool to help a child deal with fears and other challenging emotions. Plus, mindsight exercises lead to integration, because as you know, where we focus our attention, neurons fire and become active, then wire to other neurons. In this case, when Andrea helped Nicole focus on her breath, she was not only addressing her feelings of anxiety. She was also helping her daughter return to her hub, so she could notice other parts of herself and even physical sensations that she could then intentionally change. So her neurons associated with mindfully focusing on her breath became wired to her neurons related to feelings of calm and well-being. She moved into a completely new state of mind and was able to get back to her hub.

While this example focuses on an older, school-age child, younger kids can benefit from mindsight exercises as well. Even as young as four or five, kids can learn to focus on their breath. A good technique is to have them lie down and place a toy—like a boat—on their stomach. Ask them to focus on the boat, watching it rise and fall as it rides the waves of breath.

But we're not suggesting that mindsight exercises require a

INSTEAD OF DISMISS AND DENY...

...EXERCISE MINDSIGHT

person to lie down and enter a meditative state. One of the best tools you give your kids for when they feel anxious or afraid, or even when they're having trouble falling asleep, is to teach them to visualize a place where they feel calm and peaceful: floating on a raft in a pool, sitting next to a river they remember from a camping trip, or swinging in a hammock at their grandparents' house.

Mindsight exercises lead to *survival* which can help kids manage their anxieties, frustrations, and, for older children, even intense anger. But these strategies lead to *thriving* as well. After Andrea introduced Nicole to the mindsight exercise before her recital (where she ultimately relaxed and played beautifully), they returned to similar exercises from time to time, with Andrea leading Nicole through certain visualizations like the one above. As she grew older and kept practicing, Nicole began to understand more about the hub of her wheel, so she could get back to it more easily and quickly. She learned to focus more precisely and specifically on the parts of herself that she wanted to develop and grow.

Watch for ways to help your children learn to be still and calm at times and find the deep-ocean peacefulness within their hub. From there they'll be better able to survive the storms brewing within them from moment to moment, and they'll have a better chance of thriving—emotionally, psychologically, socially—as they grow toward adulthood.

Whole-Brain Kids:
Teach Your Kids About Integrating the Many Parts of Themselves

We've already given you several examples of how other parents have introduced their children to mindsight and the power of focused attention. Here is something you can read with your own child to teach the concept.

CHOOSING WHAT YOU THINK ABOUT

DO YOU EVER FEEL LIKE YOU "GET STUCK" ON A FEELING OR A THOUGHT? MAYBE AN UNHAPPY ONE THAT'S SO POWERFUL IT MAKES YOU FORGET ABOUT OTHER FEELINGS AND THOUGHTS THAT MAKE YOU HAPPY OR EXCITED?

THE GOOD NEWS IS THAT YOU DON'T HAVE TO STAY STUCK ON FEELINGS THAT UPSET YOU. YOU CAN LEARN TO FOCUS ON OTHER PARTS OF YOURSELF AND GET UNSTUCK.

FOR EXAMPLE:

NASSIM COULDN'T STOP THINKING ABOUT THE SPELLING BEE. HE EVEN HAD A STOMACHACHE. HE DIDN'T FEEL LIKE EATING HIS LUNCH OR PLAYING AT RECESS. ALL HE COULD THINK ABOUT WAS SPELL- ING. HE WAS NERVOUS.

THEN HIS TEACHER, MS. ANDERSON, TAUGHT HIM ABOUT HIS WHEEL OF AWARENESS. SHE EXPLAINED THAT OUR MINDS ARE LIKE A BICYCLE WHEEL. AT THE CENTER OF THE WHEEL, CALLED THE HUB, IS OUR SAFE PLACE WHERE OUR MIND CAN RELAX AND CHOOSE WHAT IT THINKS ABOUT.

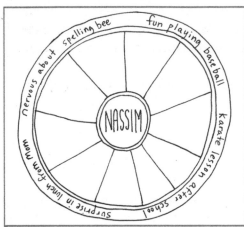

ON THE RIM OF THE WHEEL ARE ALL THE THINGS NASSIM COULD THINK ABOUT AND FEEL: HOW HE LIKES PLAYING BASEBALL AT RECESS, WHAT SURPRISE HIS MOM COULD HAVE PACKED IN HIS LUNCH, AND, OF COURSE, HIS NERVOUSNESS ABOUT THE SPELLING BEE. SHE EXPLAINED THAT HE WAS ONLY FOCUSING ON THE NERVOUSNESS POINT ON HIS RIM AND IGNORING THE OTHER PARTS.

MS. ANDERSON HAD NASSIM CLOSE HIS EYES AND TAKE THREE DEEP BREATHS. SHE SAID, "YOU'VE BEEN FOCUSING ON YOUR WORRIES ABOUT SPELLING. NOW I WANT YOU TO FOCUS ON THE PART OF YOUR WHEEL THAT HAS FUN PLAYING BASEBALL, AND THE PART THAT CAN IMAGINE A YUMMY LUNCH." HE SMILED AND HIS STOMACH STARTED TO GRUMBLE.

WHEN NASSIM OPENED HIS EYES HE FELT BETTER. HE HAD USED HIS WHEEL OF AWARENESS TO FOCUS ON OTHER FEELINGS AND THOUGHTS, AND HE HAD CHANGED HOW HE FELT. HE WAS STILL A LITTLE NERVOUS, BUT HE WASN'T STUCK ON <u>JUST</u> THE NERVOUSNESS.

HE LEARNED THAT HE DOESN'T HAVE TO THINK ONLY ABOUT NERVOUS FEELINGS, AND THAT HE CAN USE HIS MIND TO THINK ABOUT OTHER THINGS THAT CAN HELP HIM HAVE FUN AND NOT FEEL SO WORRIED. NASSIM ATE HIS LUNCH AND RAN OUTSIDE TO PLAY BASEBALL.

Integrating Ourselves: Looking at Our Own Wheel of Awareness

There are many ways parents can benefit from an understanding of mindsight and their own wheel of awareness. Let's take a moment so you can see, and experience, what we're talking about.

From your hub, SIFT through your own mind. What rim points have your attention right now? Maybe some of these?

- I'm so tired. I wish I had just one more hour of sleep.
- I'm also irritated that my son's Yankees cap is there on the floor. Now when he gets home I'll have to ride him about that, *and* about his homework.
- Dinner with the Coopers will be fun tonight, but I kind of wish we weren't going.
- I'm tired.
- I wish I did more for myself. At least I'm giving myself the pleasure of reading a book these days.
- Did I mention I'm tired?

All of these sensations, images, feelings, and thoughts are the rim points on your wheel of awareness, and together they determine your state of mind.

Now let's see what happens when you intentionally direct your attention to other rim points. Slow down for a few seconds, get quiet within yourself, and ask yourself these questions:

- What's something funny or adorable my child said or did lately?
- Even though it's monstrously difficult at times, do I genuinely love and appreciate getting to be a parent? How would I feel if I didn't get to be a parent?
- What's my child's favorite T-shirt right now? Can I remember her first pair of shoes?
- Can I picture how my child might look at eighteen, bags packed and leaving for college?

Feeling different? Has your state of mind changed?

Mindsight did that. From your hub you noticed the rim points on your own wheel of awareness, and you became aware of what you were experiencing. Then you shifted your focus, directing your attention to other rim points, and as a result, your entire state of mind changed. *This is the power of your mind, and this is how it can literally and fundamentally transform the way you feel about and interact with your kids.* Without mindsight, you can get stuck on your rim, feeling primarily frustrated or angry or resentful. The joy of parenting is gone in

[BOX CONTINUES ON NEXT PAGE]

that moment. But by returning to your hub and shifting your focus, you can begin to experience joy and gratitude about getting to parent your children—just by paying attention and *deciding* to direct your attention to new rim points.

Mindsight can also be immensely practical. For example, think for a moment right now about the last time you got angry with one of your children. Really angry, where you could've lost control. Remember what he did, and how furious you felt. At times like these, the anger you feel burns bright and fiery on the rim of your wheel. In fact, it burns so intensely that it far outshines other rim points that represent the feelings and knowledge you have about your kids: your understanding that your four-year-old is acting like a normal four-year-old; your memory of laughing hysterically together, just a few minutes earlier, as you played cards; the promise you made that you were going to stop grabbing your children's arms when you're angry; your desire to model appropriate expressions of anger.

This is how we become swept up by the rim when we're not integrated via the hub. The downstairs brain takes over any integrative functioning of the upstairs area, and other rim points are eclipsed by the glare of this single point of your all-consuming anger. Remember "flipping your lid"?

What do you need to do in a moment like this? Yep, you guessed it: integrate. Use your mindsight. By focusing on your breath, you can at least begin to get back to the hub of your mind. This is the required step that allows us to pull back from being consumed by a single angry point on the rim—or a few of them. Once in the hub, it becomes possible to take in the wider perspective that there are other rim points to keep in mind. You can get some water, take a break and stretch, or give yourself a moment to collect yourself. Then, once you've brought your attention back to your hub, you'll be free to choose how you want to respond to your child and if necessary repair any breach in your relationship.

This doesn't mean ignoring bad behavior. Not at all. In fact, one of the rim points you'll integrate with the others is your belief in setting clear and consistent boundaries. There are many perspectives you can embrace, from desires for your child to act in a different way to feelings of concern over how you've acted in response. When you link all these different rim points together—when you've used the hub to integrate your mind at that moment—you'll feel a readiness to continue attuned, sensitive parenting. Then, with your whole brain working together, you can connect with your child because you are connected within yourself. You'll have a much better chance of responding the way you want to, with mindsight and the wholeness of who you are, instead of an immediate reaction spurred on by a fiery point on the rim of your wheel. To do your own wheel practice, go to drdansiegel.com.

CHAPTER 6

The Me-We Connection

Integrating Self and Other

Ron and Sandy were fed up. Their seven-year-old, Colin, was a good kid. He didn't cause trouble at school, his friends and their parents liked him, and he generally did what he was supposed to do. But he was, in his parents' words, "totally and incurably selfish." He always grabbed the last slice of pizza, even if he still had some on his plate. He begged for a puppy, then showed no interest in even playing with it, much less using the pooper scooper. Even after growing out of his toys, he still refused to let his younger brother play with them.

Ron and Sandy knew that a certain amount of egocentrism in children is normal. And they didn't want to change Colin's personality—they wanted to love him for who he was. But at times it drove them crazy that he often seemed incapable of thinking about other people. When it came to relational skills like empathy, kindness, and consideration, Colin just seemed to be missing the development of that circuit.

The breaking point came one day after school when Colin disappeared into the bedroom he shared with his five-year-old brother, Logan. Ron was in the kitchen when he heard yelling from the boys' room. He went to investigate and discovered a distraught Logan, furious with his big brother and crying over a pile of artwork and trophies. Colin had decided to "redecorate" the room. He had taken down all of Logan's watercolor paintings and marker drawings hanging on the walls and replaced them with his own posters and baseball cards, which he'd taped in rows across the largest wall in the room. In addition, he had removed Logan's two soccer trophies from the shelf and set up his own bobblehead dolls in their place. Colin had piled all of Logan's belongings in a corner of the room, he explained, "so they wouldn't be in the way."

When Sandy got home she and Ron talked about their frustration with their older son. They sincerely believed that there was no malice in Colin's actions. In fact, that was almost the problem: he never even *considered* Logan's feelings enough to intend to hurt him. He redecorated the room for the same reason he always took the last slice of pizza: he just didn't think about others.

This issue is a common one for parents. We want our kids to be caring and considerate so they can enjoy meaningful relationships. Sometimes we fear that because they're not as kind (or compassionate or grateful or generous) as we want them to be, they never will be. Of course, we can't expect a seven-year-old to behave as if he were an enlightened adult. Sure, we want our kids to become men and women who are strong and forgiving and respectful and loving, but that's a bit much to expect of someone who's just recently learned to tie his shoes.

However, while it's important to trust the process and know that much of what we want for our kids will emerge only over time, we *can* prepare them and steer them toward becoming children, teens, and ultimately adults who are fully capable of participating in relationships and considering the feelings of others. Some people simply have fewer neural connections in their circuitry in charge of empathy and relationships. Just like kids who have trouble reading need to practice and grow those connections in their brain, kids who have difficulty relating to others need to have those connections encouraged and cultivated. And just as a learning disability is a sign of a mental challenge, so is an inability to feel someone else's pain. It's a developmental issue, not necessarily a character problem. Even children who don't seem predisposed to connection and compassion can *learn* what it means to be in relationship, and to fulfill the responsibilities that come with it.

That's what this chapter is about. Most of the information we've provided in earlier chapters focuses on how to help develop your child's whole brain in order to develop a strong and resilient sense of "me." But like Ron and Sandy, you know that kids need just as much help understanding what it means to become part of a "we," so that they can be integrated with others. In fact, in our ever-changing modern society, learning to move from "me" to "we" may be essential for how our children will be able to adapt in our future world.

Helping children become a participating member of a "we" while not losing touch with their individual "me" is a tall order for any parent. But happiness and fulfillment result from being connected to others while still maintaining a unique identity. That's also the essence of mindsight, which you'll remember is all about seeing your own mind, as well as the mind of another. It's about developing fulfilling relationships while maintaining a healthy sense of self.

In the previous chapter we discussed the first aspect of mindsight, seeing and understanding our own mind. We talked about helping kids become aware of and integrate the many different parts of themselves via the wheel of awareness. The key concept in this aspect of mindsight is personal *insight*.

Now we want to turn our attention to the second aspect of mindsight, developing the ability to see and connect with the minds of others. This connection depends on *empathy*, on recognizing the feelings, desires, and perspectives of another. Ron and Sandy's son seemed to need empathy skills. In addition to developing and integrating his whole brain and the different parts of himself, he needed to be given lots of practice at seeing things from other people's perspectives, seeing other people's minds. He needed to develop this second aspect of mindsight.

Insight + Empathy = Mindsight

Insight and empathy. If we can encourage these attributes in our kids, we will give them the gift of mindsight, offering them awareness about themselves, and connection with those around them. But how do we do that? How do we encourage our kids to connect with family, friends, and the world while cultivating and maintaining their own individual sense of self? How do we help them learn to share? To get along with siblings? To negotiate playground politics? To communicate well and consider others' feelings? The answers to all these questions emerge from the me-we connection, which we can understand by first looking at how the brain participates in the creation of relationships.

The Social Brain: Wired for "We"

What do you picture when you think about the brain? Maybe you recall an image from high school biology class: that weird organ floating in the jar, or a picture of it in a textbook. The problem with this "single skull" perspective—where we consider each individual brain as a lone organ isolated in a single skull—is that it neglects the truth that scientists have come to understand over the last few decades: that the brain is a social organ, made to be in relationship. It's hardwired to take in signals from the social environment, which in turn influence a person's inner world. In other words, what happens *between* brains has a great deal to do with what happens *within* each individual brain. Self and community are fundamentally interrelated, since every brain is continually constructed by its interactions with others. Even more, studies of happiness and wisdom reveal that a key factor in well-being is devoting one's attention and passions to the benefit of others instead of just focusing on the individual, separate concerns of a private self. The "me" discovers meaning and happiness by joining and belonging to a "we."

To put it differently, the brain is set up for *interpersonal integration*. Just as its many different parts are made to work together, each individual brain is made to relate with the brain of each person we interact with. Interpersonal integration means that we honor and nurture our differences while cultivating our connections with one another. So while we want to help our kids integrate their left and right brain, their upstairs and downstairs brain, their implicit and explicit memories, and so on, we also need to help them understand the extent to which they are connected to their family, friends, classmates, and other people in their communities. By understanding basic facets of the relational brain, we can help our kids develop the mindsight that will allow them to enjoy deeper and more meaningful relationships.

MIRROR NEURONS: THE REFLECTORS IN THE MIND

Do you ever get thirsty when you see someone take a drink? Or yawn when someone else does? These familiar responses can be understood in light of one of the most fascinating recent discoveries about the brain: mirror neurons. Here's how the discovery took place.

In the early 1990s, a group of Italian neuroscientists were studying the brain of a macaque monkey. They had implanted electrodes to monitor individual neurons, and when the monkey ate a peanut, a certain electrode fired. No surprise there—that's what the researchers expected. But then a scientist's snack changed the course of our insight into the mind. One of the researchers picked up a peanut and ate it as the monkey watched. In response, the monkey's motor neuron fired—the same one that had fired when he had actually eaten the peanut himself! The researchers discovered that the monkey's brain was influenced and became active just by *watching* the actions of another. Whether the monkey witnessed an action or performed that same behavior himself, the same set of neurons became activated.

Scientists immediately began scrambling to identify these "mirror neurons" in humans. And while there are far more questions than answers about exactly what they are and how they work, we are actively learning more and more about the mirror neuron system. These neurons may be the root of empathy, and therefore contribute to mindsight, in the human brain.

The key is that mirror neurons respond only to an act with intention, where there's some predictability or purpose that can be perceived. For example, if someone simply waves her hand in the air randomly, your mirror neurons won't respond. But if that person carries out an act you can predict from experience, like taking a drink from a cup of water, your mirror neurons will "figure out" what's intended before the person does it. So when she lifts up her hand with a cup in it, you can predict at a synaptic level that she intends to drink from it. Not only that, the mirror neurons in your own upstairs brain will get you ready to drink as well. We see an act, we understand the purpose of the act, and we ready ourselves to mirror it.

At the simplest level, that's why we get thirsty when others drink, and why we yawn when others yawn. It may be why even a newborn infant, just a few hours old, can mimic his parents when he sticks out his tongue. Mirror neurons may also explain why younger siblings are sometimes better at sports. Before they ever join their own team, their mirror neurons have fired each of the hundreds of times they've watched their older siblings hit, kick, and throw a ball. At the most complex level, mirror neurons help us understand the nature of culture and how our shared behaviors bind us together, child to parent, friend to friend, and eventually spouse to spouse.

Now let's take another step. Based on what we see (as well as hear, smell, touch, and taste) in the world around us, we can mirror not only the behavioral intentions of others, but also their emotional states. In other words, mirror neurons may allow us not only to imitate others' behaviors, but actually to resonate with their feelings. We sense not only what action is coming next, but also the emotion that underlies the behavior. For this reason, we could also call these special neural cells "sponge neurons" in that we soak up like a sponge what we see in the behaviors, intentions, and emotions of someone else. We don't just "mirror back" to someone else, but we "sponge in" their internal states.

Notice what happens when you're at a party with friends. If you approach a group that's laughing, you'll probably find yourself smiling or chuckling even before you've heard the joke. Or have you noticed that when you're nervous or stressed out, your kids will often be that way, too? Scientists call this "emotional contagion." The internal states of others—from joy and playfulness to sadness and fear—directly affect our own state of mind. We soak other people into our own inner world.

You can see, then, why neuroscientists call the brain a social organ. It's absolutely built for mindsight. We are biologically equipped to be in relationships, to understand where other people are coming from, and to influence one another. As we've explained throughout the book, the brain is actually reshaped by our experiences. That means that every discussion, argument, joke, or hug we share with someone else literally alters our brain and that of the other person. After a powerful conversation or time spent with an important person in our life, we have a different brain. Since none of us is working from a single-skull mind, our whole mental life results from our inner neural world and the external signals we receive from others. Each of us is meant to join our individual "me" with others to become a part of "we."

Laying the Groundwork for Connection: Creating Positive Mental Models

What does all this mean for our children? The kinds of relationships they experience will lay the groundwork for how they relate to others for the rest of their lives. In other words, how well they'll be able to use their mindsight to participate in a "we" and join with others down the road is based on the quality of their attachment relationships with their caregivers—including parents and grandparents, but also significant babysitters, teachers, peers, and other influential people in their lives.

When kids spend time with the most important people in their life, they develop important relational skills like communicating and listening well, interpreting facial expressions, understanding nonverbal communication, sharing, and sacrificing. But also, in relationships, children develop models about how they themselves fit into the world around them, and how relationships work. They learn whether they can trust others to see and respond to their needs, and whether they feel connected and protected enough to step out and take risks. In short, they learn whether relationships will leave them feeling alone and unseen; anxious and confused; or felt, understood, and securely cared for.

Think of a newborn. A baby is born ready to connect, ready to link what she sees in others with what she does and with what she feels inside. But what if those others are only rarely attuned to what she needs? What if, more often than not, her parents are unavailable and rejecting? Then confusion and frustration will initially permeate the child's mind. Without intimate moments of consistent connection with her caregivers, she may grow up without mindsight, without an understanding of the importance of joining with someone else. We learn early in life to use our connections with reliable others to soothe our internal distress. This is the basis of secure attachment. But if we aren't given such nurturing, our brain will need to adapt and do the best it can. Children can learn to "go it alone" in an effort to soothe themselves as best they can. The relational, emotional circuitry of this child's brain, which needs closeness and connection that are not being offered to her, may completely shut down as a way of adapting. This is how the social brain shuts down its innate drive for connection just to survive. However, if her parents can learn to show her consistent, predictable love and attunement, she will develop mindsight and live up to the relational potential her brain has been wired for.

It's not just parents who create the strategies of adaptation—or mental models—for how children view relationships. Think about what your children are learning from their relationships with various caregivers, like the coach who emphasizes the importance of working together and making sacrifices for teammates. Or the aunt who is hypercritical, who teaches that a central part of a relationship involves disapproval and finding fault. Or the classmate who views all relationships through the lens of competition, seeing everyone as a rival or adversary. Or the teacher who emphasizes kindness and mutual respect and models compassion in her interactions with the children in her class.

All of these different relational experiences wire a child's brain for what a "we" feels like. Remember that the brain uses repeated experiences or associations to predict what to expect. When relationships are cold and people are essentially distant, critical, or competitive, that influences what the child expects relationships to feel like. On the other hand, if the child experiences relationships full of nurturing warmth, connection, and protection, then that will become the model for future relationships—with friends, with other members of various communities, and eventually with romantic partners and their own children.

It's really not an exaggeration to say that the kind of relationships you provide for your children will affect generations to come. We can impact the future of the world by caring well for our children and by being intentional in giving them the kinds of relationships that we value and that we want them to see as normal.

Preparing for "We": Offering Experiences That Lead to Connection

In addition to modeling good relationships for our kids, we need to prepare them to join with others, so they'll be capable of becoming a part of a "we." After all, just because the mind is equipped and designed to connect with others doesn't mean that a child is born with relationship skills. Being born with muscles doesn't make you an athlete: you need to learn and practice specific skills. Likewise, children don't emerge from the womb wanting to share their toys. Nor are their first words "I'll sacrifice what I want so we can strike a mutually beneficial compromise." On the contrary, the phrases that dominate the vocabulary of toddlers— "mine," "me," and even "no"—emphasize their lack of understanding of what it means to be a part of a "we." So they have to *learn* mindsight skills like sharing, forgiving, sacrifice, and listening.

Colin, Ron and Sandy's son who seems so egocentric, is for the most part a very normal kid. He just hasn't quite mastered many of the mindsight skills that are necessary for participating as a contributing member of a family. His parents' expectation was that by the time he was seven, he'd be more integrated into the family and willing to be a part of a "we." While he's steadily improving his relational intelligence, he needs practice to keep moving in that direction.

The same goes for a shy child. Lisa, a mom we know, has pictures of one of her sons at his friend's fourth-birthday party. All of the children are gathered in a tight circle around a young woman dressed like Dora the Explorer. All, that is, except for Lisa's son Ian, who insisted on standing six feet away from the circle of not-so-shy kids. It was the same at his toddler music class. While the other children sang and danced and itsy-bitsy-spidered their little hands off, Ian sat in his mom's lap and refused to do anything more than timidly observe.

In those years, Lisa and her husband had to walk the line between encouraging new relationships and pushing too hard. But by giving their son repeated opportunities to interact with other children and to figure out how to make friends, all while supporting and comforting him when he was nervous or afraid, they helped their young introvert develop the social skills he needed. And while these days Ian is still not quick to dive headfirst into new social situations, he is very comfortable with himself, and even outgoing at times. He looks people in the eye when he talks to them, raises his hand in class, and is even frequently the ringleader in the dugout for a (very enthusiastic) rendition of "Take Me Out to the Ball Game."

Researchers who study human personality tell us that shyness is to a large extent genetic. It's actually a part of a person's core makeup present at birth. However, as in the case of Ian, that doesn't mean that shyness isn't changeable to a significant degree. In fact, the way parents handle their child's shyness has a big impact on how the child deals with that aspect of his or her personality, as well as how shy the child is later on.

The point is that parenting matters, even to the extent of influencing our inborn and genetically shaped temperament. We can help prepare our kids to join with others and experience meaningful relationships by offering encouragement and opportunities that help them develop those mindsight skills. We'll talk in a minute about some specific ways to do that. But first let's explain what we mean by helping kids be receptive to being in relationships.

CULTIVATING A "YES" STATE OF MIND: HELPING KIDS BE RECEPTIVE TO RELATIONSHIPS

If we want to prepare kids to participate as healthy individuals in a relationship, we need to create within them an *open, receptive* state, instead of a *closed, reactive* one. To illustrate, here's an exercise Dan uses with many families. First he'll tell them he's going to repeat a word several times, and he asks them just to notice what it feels like in their bodies. The first word is "no," said firmly and slightly harshly seven times, with about two seconds between each "no." Then, after another pause, he says a clear but somewhat gentler "yes" seven times. Afterward, clients often say that the "no" felt stifling and angering, as if they were being shut down or scolded. In contrast, the "yes" made them feel calm, peaceful, even light. (You might close your eyes now and try the exercise for yourself. Notice what goes on in your body as you or a friend says "no" and then "yes" several times.)

These two different responses—the "no" feelings and the "yes" feelings—demonstrate what we mean when we talk about reactivity versus receptivity. When the nervous system is *reactive,* it's actually in a fight-flight-freeze response state, from which it's almost impossible to connect in an open and caring way with another person. Remember the amygdala and the other parts of your downstairs brain that react immediately, without thinking, whenever you feel threatened? When our entire focus is on self-defense, no matter what we do, we stay in that reactive, "no" state of mind. We become guarded, unable to join with someone else—by listening well, by giving them the benefit of the doubt, by considering their feelings, and so on. Even neutral comments can transform into fighting words, distorting what we hear to fit what we fear. This is how we enter a reactive state and prepare to fight, to flee, or even to freeze.

On the other hand, when we're receptive, a different set of circuits in the brain becomes active. The "yes" part of the exercise, for most people, produces a positive experience. The muscles of their face and vocal cords relax, their blood pressure and heart rate normalize, and they become more open to experiencing whatever another person wants to express. In short, they become more receptive. Whereas reactivity emerges from our downstairs brain and leaves us feeling shut down, upset, and defensive, a receptive state turns on the social engagement system that involves a different set of circuits of the upstairs brain that connects us to others, allowing us to feel safe and seen.

When interacting with our kids, it can be extremely helpful to decipher whether they're in a reactive or receptive state of mind. This of course requires mindsight on our part. We need to consider where our kids are emotionally (and where we ourselves are) at any given moment. If your four-year-old is screaming "I wanna swing longer!" as you carry her under one arm away from the park, that may not be the best time to talk to her about appropriate ways of handling big emotions. Wait until this reactive state passes; then, when she's more receptive, talk to her about how you'd like to see her respond the next time she's disappointed. Likewise, when your eleven-year-old finds out that he didn't get accepted into the art program he'd set his heart on, you may need to hold off on word-heavy pronouncements of hope and alternatives. The downstairs state of reactivity doesn't know what to do with a lot of upstairs words. Often, in moments of reactivity, nonverbals (like hugs and empathetic facial expressions) will be much more powerful.

Over time, we want to help our children become more receptive to relationships, and help them develop mindsight skills that will let them join with others. Then receptivity can lead to resonance—a way of joining from the inside out—that will allow them to enjoy the depth and intimacy that come with meaningful relationships. Otherwise, a child is left adrift, motivated by a sense of isolation rather than a desire and ability to join.

One final note before we turn to steps we can take to encourage receptivity and relational skills: as we help children be more receptive to joining with others, we need to keep in mind the importance of maintaining their individual identity as well. For a ten-year-old girl who's doing everything within her power to fit in with a clique of mean girls at school, the problem may not be that she's not receptive enough to joining a "we." The concern for her may be just the opposite, that she's lost sight of her "me" and is therefore going along with everything this set of bullies tells her to do. Any healthy relationship—whether it's family, friendship, romantic, or otherwise—is made up of healthy individuals in connection with others. To become a part of a well-functioning "we," a person needs also to remain an individual "me." Just as we don't want our kids to be only right-brained or only left-brained, we also don't want them to be only individualistic, leaving them selfish and isolated, or only relational, leaving them needy, dependent, and vulnerable to unhealthy and harmful relationships. We want them to be whole-brained, and enjoy integrated relationships.

What You Can Do:
Helping Your Child Integrate Self and Other

Whole-Brain Strategy #11:
Increase the Family Fun Factory: Making a Point to Enjoy Each Other

Do you ever feel like you're spending most of your time either disciplining the kids or carting them from one activity to the next, and not enough time just enjoying being with them? If you do, you're not alone; most of us feel this from time to time. Sometimes it's easy to forget to just have fun as a family. Yet we are hardwired for play and exploration as well as for joining with one another. In fact, "playful parenting" is one of the best ways to prepare your children for relationships and encourage them to connect with others. That's because it gives them positive experiences being with the people they spend the most time with: their parents.

Of course children need structure and boundaries and to be held accountable for their behavior, but even as you maintain your authority, don't forget to have fun with your kids. Play games. Tell jokes. Be silly. Take an interest in what they care about. The more they enjoy the time they spend with you and the rest of the family, the more they'll value relationships and desire more positive and healthy relational experiences in the future.

The reason is simple. With every fun, enjoyable experience you give your children while they are with the family, you provide them with positive reinforcement about what it means to be in loving relationship with others. One reason has to do with a chemical in your brain called dopamine. Dopamine is a neurotransmitter, which means that it enables communication between brain cells. Your brain cells receive what some people call "dopamine squirts" when something pleasurable happens to you, and it motivates you to want to do it again. Scientists who study addiction point to these dopamine surges as factors that lead people to maintain a certain habit or addiction, even when they know it's bad for them. But we can also help produce dopamine squirts that reinforce positive and healthy desires, like enjoying family relationships. Dopamine is the chemical of reward—and play and fun are rewarding in our lives.

What this means is that when your son squeals in delight when you dramatically "die" from his Peter Pan sword thrust, when you and your daughter dance together at a concert or in the living room, or when you and your kids work together on a gardening or construction project, the experience strengthens the bonds between you and teaches your kids that relationships are affirming, rewarding, and fulfilling. So give it a shot, maybe even tonight. After dinner, call out, "Everybody take your plate back to the kitchen, then find one blanket and meet me in the living room. We're having Popsicles in a fort tonight!"

Another fun family activity that also teaches receptivity is to play improv games together. The basic concept is similar to what improv comedians do when the audience gives them suggestions and the comedians have to take the random ideas and combine them in funny ways that make some sort of sense. If you and your kids are performers, you can actually do this kind of improv together. But there are simpler versions of the activity as well. Let someone begin a story, then after one sentence, the next person has to add to it, followed by the next person, and so on. Games and activities like these not only keep the family fun factor high, but also give kids practice at being receptive to the unexpected turns life presents them. You don't want to turn the game into a serious classroom experience, but watch for ways to explicitly connect what you're doing to the concept of receptivity. Spontaneity and creativity are important abilities, and novelty also gets dopamine going.

The fun-factor principle also applies to the experiences you give your kids as siblings. Recent studies have found that the best predictor for good sibling relationships later in life is how much fun the kids have together when they're young. The rate of conflict can even be high, as long as there's plenty of fun to balance it out. The real danger comes when the siblings just ignore each other. There may be less tension to deal with, but that's also a recipe for a cold and distant relationship as adults.

So if you want to develop close long-term relationships between your kids, think of it as a math equation, where the amount of enjoyment they share together should be greater than the conflict they experience. You're never going to get the conflict side of the equation to zero. Siblings argue; they just do. But if you can increase the other side of the equation, giving them activities that produce positive emotions and memories, you'll create strong bonds between them and set up a relationship that has a good chance of remaining solid for life.

Some sibling fun will occur naturally, but you can help it along, too. Break out a new box of sidewalk chalk and have them create a crazy new monster together. Let them use the video camera to make a movie. Have them team up together for a surprise project to give to a grandparent. However you do it—family bike rides, board games, making cookies, teaming up against Mom with the water guns, whatever—find ways to help your kids have fun together and strengthen the bonds that connect them.

You can also use fun, and even silliness, to shift your children's state of mind when they become stuck in an angry or defiant state. Sometimes they won't be in the mood to have you act silly or playful, so be sensitive to the cues you receive, especially with older kids. But if you're sensitive to how your playfulness will be received, this can be an extremely powerful and easily implemented way to help children shift how they are feeling.

Your state of mind can influence your child's state of mind, letting you transform fussiness and irritability into fun, laughter, and connection.

INSTEAD OF COMMAND AND DEMAND...

...TRY PLAYFUL PARENTING

Whole-Brain Strategy #12:
Connection Through Conflict: Teach Kids to Argue with a
"We" in Mind

We might wish we could somehow help our kids avoid all conflict, but we can't. If they're going to be in relationships, they're going to face quarrels and disagreements. We can, though, teach them some basic mindsight skills so they'll know how to manage conflict in healthy and productive ways, and respond when things don't go perfectly as they interact with others.

Once again, each new disagreement is more than just a difficulty to survive. It represents another opportunity for you to teach your children important lessons so they can thrive, in this case relationally. Handling conflict well isn't easy, even for adults, so we can't expect too much of our children. But there are some simple skills we can teach them that will help us all survive individual conflicts, as well as help our children thrive as they move toward adulthood. Let's look at three of these mindsight-building skills.

See Through the Other Person's Eyes: Help Kids Recognize Other Points of View

Does this scenario sound familiar? You're working at your desk and your seven-year-old daughter approaches. She's clearly angry. She announces that her younger brother, Mark, just called her stupid. You ask why he might have said that, and your daughter is adamant that there's no reason—he just said it!

It can be difficult for any of us to see things from someone else's perspective. We see what we see, and often only what we *want* to see. But the more we can use our mindsight to view events through the eyes of another, the better chance we have of resolving conflict in a healthy manner.

That's a tough skill to teach children, especially in the middle of a heated argument. But if we ourselves can remain aware of what we're actually saying, we have a better chance of teaching the lessons we want. For example, your inclination might be to say, "Well, what did you do to Mark? I'm sure he didn't just call you stupid out of the blue!"

INSTEAD OF DISMISS AND DENY...

...TRY CONNECTION THROUGH CONFLICT

But if you can remain calm and aware of what you want to teach, you might go at the conversation a bit differently. First you'd want to demonstrate an awareness of your daughter's feelings. (Remember, connect first, then redirect.) This will decrease your daughter's defensiveness and prepare her to see how her brother feels. Then you could aim for the goal of creating some empathy in your daughter.

Granted, we won't always get through to our kids. But by asking questions about how another person feels, about why someone reacted as he did, we can encourage empathy in our children. The act of considering the mind of another requires us to use our right hemisphere and our upstairs brain, both of which are part of the social circuitry that allows us to enjoy mature and fulfilling relationships.

Listen to What's Not Being Said:
Teach Kids About Nonverbal Communication and Attuning to Others

It's great that we teach our children to pay attention to what people are saying: "Listen to his words. He said he didn't *want* to be sprayed by the hose!" But an important part of relationships is listening to what's *not* being said. Usually kids aren't naturally skilled at this. That's why, when you reprimand your son for making his little sister cry by dipping his pretzels into her yogurt, he responds, "But she likes it! We're playing a game."

Nonverbal clues sometimes communicate even more than words, so we need to help our children use their right hemisphere to get good at understanding what other people are saying, even if they never open their mouth. With the mirror neuron system already working, all kids need is for us to help them make explicit what their mirror neurons are communicating. For example, after winning a big soccer game, your son might need you to help him notice that his friend on the other team is in need of some cheering up, even if he says he's fine. As evidence, you can point to the friend's body language and facial expressions—the drooping shoulders, the lowered head, the downcast face. By helping your son make these simple observations you'll increase his mindsight, and for the rest of his life he'll be better equipped to read others and tune in to their feelings.

Repair: Teach Kids to Make Things Right After a Conflict

We know the importance of apologizing, and we teach our children to say they're sorry. But kids also need to realize that at times, that's only the beginning. Sometimes they need to take steps to right whatever they've done wrong.

The situation might call for a specific, direct response: repairing or replacing a broken toy, or helping to rebuild some sort of project. Or a more relational response might be warranted, like drawing the other person a picture, performing an act of kindness, or writing a letter of apology. The point is that you're helping your kids demonstrate acts of love and contrition that show they've thought about another's feelings and want to find a way to repair the rupture in the relationship.

This connects directly to the two whole-brain strategies above, about empathy and attuning to others' feelings. To sincerely want to make things right, a child must understand how the other person is feeling and why that person is upset. Then the parent can more profitably bring up the question "If it were you and your favorite thing were broken, what would help you feel better?" Each new movement toward considering someone else's feelings creates stronger connections in the relational circuitry of the brain. When we break through our children's defensiveness and their reluctance to accept responsibility, we can help them be thoughtful about others they've hurt, and make an effort toward reconnection. We help them develop mindsight. Sometimes a sincere apology is enough, especially when combined with honesty and sincerity: "I did that because I was feeling jealous, and I'm sorry." But kids also need to learn what it means to go the extra mile and take specific steps toward reconciliation.

Let's return to Colin, the seven-year-old whose parents felt he was too selfish. We wish we could offer Ron and Sandy some sort of magic bullet, a cure-all for egocentrism and other developmental frustrations they encounter with their son. But obviously we can't. The good news, though, is that simply by loving Colin and helping him see the benefits of relationships—beginning with his interactions with his parents and brother—Ron and Sandy are already helping him understand the importance of considering and connecting with others.

Beyond that, by emphasizing the "connection through conflict" skills we're discussing here, they can help him continue moving toward considering the feelings of others. For example, when Colin redecorated his room and removed his brother's belongings, this presented a teachable moment, which his parents could use to help Colin learn a lot about being in relationship. Too often we forget that "discipline" really means "to teach"—not "to punish." A disciple is a student, not a recipient of behavioral consequences. When we teach mindsight, we take moments of conflict and transform them into opportunities for learning, skill building, and brain development.

In that moment, Ron could ask Colin to look at his brother, crying as he picked up and straightened out his various paintings, and notice the nonverbal evidence of how hurt Logan was. This could lead to a thoughtful discussion about how Logan viewed the scene—the crumpled paintings, the thrown-aside trophies. Simply getting Colin to actually see Logan's perspective would be a pretty big breakthrough with long-lasting benefits. A mere time-out might or might not teach Colin not to remove his brother's things without permission, but it wouldn't generalize into a mindsight skill.

Finally, Ron and Sandy could discuss what should happen to make things right, including having Colin apologize and work with Logan to create some new paintings to hang on the shared wall in the room. By choosing to use the situation for growth and teaching, rather than avoiding it as an unpleasant obstacle, Colin's parents could convert some fairly intense conflict into a thrive moment and help both of their sons learn important lessons about what it means to be in a relationship. The key is opening up mindsight's lens to make the perception of each boy's inner world available for inspection.

Mindsight permits children to sense the importance of the inner life of thoughts and feelings. Without such development, behaviors become just interactions a child responds to from the surface, something to "deal with" as an automatic reaction without reflection. Parents are a child's first mindsight teachers, using challenging moments to engage a child's own circuits of reflection to view our shared inner worlds. As children develop these mindsight skills, they can learn to balance the importance of their own inner lives with those of others. These reflective skills are also the basis for how children learn to balance their own emotions while understanding the emotional lives of the people around them. Mindsight is the basis of both social and emotional intelligence. It allows children to learn that they are a part of a larger world of relationships where feelings matter and connections are a source of reward, meaning, and fun.

Whole-Brain Kids:
Teach Your Kids About Integrating the Self with the Other

Now that you've learned a good bit about mindsight, here's something you can read to your own child to introduce the concept of seeing your own and each other's minds.

ME AND WE

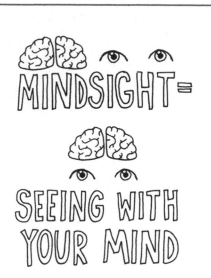

JUST LIKE "EYESIGHT" IS SEEING WITH YOUR EYES, "MINDSIGHT" IS SEEING WITH YOUR MIND. IT MEANS TWO THINGS...

FIRST, IT MEANS LOOKING INSIDE YOUR OWN MIND TO SEE WHAT'S GOING ON IN THERE. MINDSIGHT LETS YOU PAY ATTENTION TO THE PICTURES IN YOUR HEAD, THE THOUGHTS IN YOUR MIND, THE EMOTIONS YOU EXPERIENCE, AND EVEN THE FEELINGS IN YOUR BODY. IT HELPS YOU KNOW YOURSELF BETTER.

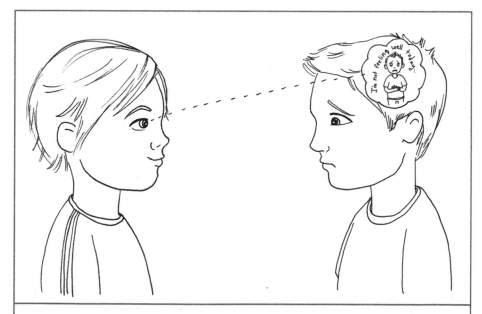

THE SECOND PART OF MINDSIGHT IS SEEING SOMEONE ELSE'S MIND AND TRYING TO LOOK AT THINGS THE WAY THEY DO.

FOR EXAMPLE:

DREW CAME HOME FROM A PLAYDATE AND TOLD HIS DAD THAT HE AND TIM HAD ARGUED OVER WHO GOT TO USE TIM'S NEW WATER GUN. THEY HAD EVENTUALLY DECIDED TO TAKE TURNS, BUT WHEN DREW GOT HOME, HE STILL FELT ANGRY.

HE EXPLAINED THAT SINCE HE WAS THE GUEST, HE FELT THAT TIM SHOULD HAVE LET HIM USE THE NEW WATER GUN. DREW'S DAD LISTENED AND SAID HE UNDERSTOOD. THEN HE ASKED, "WHY DO YOU THINK TIM WANTED TO USE IT SO MUCH?"

DREW THOUGHT FOR A SECOND. "BECAUSE IT WAS NEW, AND HE HADN'T GOTTEN TO PLAY WITH IT YET?" IN THAT MOMENT, DREW USED HIS MINDSIGHT TO UNDERSTAND TIM'S FEELINGS. HE DIDN'T FEEL AS MAD ANYMORE.

THE NEXT TIME YOU'RE UPSET WITH SOMEONE, USE YOUR OWN MINDSIGHT TO SEE HOW THE OTHER PERSON FEELS. IT CAN MAKE YOU BOTH FEEL A LOT HAPPIER.

Integrating Ourselves: Making Sense of Our Own Story

The most important "we" in your life as a parent is the relationship you share with your child. That relationship significantly impacts your child's future. Research studies have consistently shown that when parents offer repeated, predictable experiences in which they see and sensitively respond to their children's emotions and needs, their children will thrive—socially, emotionally, physically, and even academically. While it's not exactly a revelation that kids do better when they enjoy strong relationships with their parents, what may surprise you is what produces this kind of parent-child connection. It's not how our parents raised us, or how many parenting books we've read. It's actually how well we've made sense of our experiences with our own parents and how sensitive we are to our children that most powerfully influence our relationship with our kids, and therefore how well they thrive.

It all comes down to what we call our life narrative, the story we tell when we look at who we are and how we've become the person that we are. Our life narrative determines our feelings about our past, our understanding of why people (like our parents) behaved as they did, and our awareness of the way those events have impacted our development into adulthood. When we have a coherent life narrative, we have made sense of how the past has contributed to who we are and what we do.

A life narrative that hasn't been examined and made sense of may limit us in the present, and may also cause us to parent reactively and pass down to our children the same painful legacy that negatively affected our own early days. For instance, imagine that your father had a difficult childhood. Perhaps his home was an emotional desert, where his parents didn't comfort him when he was afraid or sad, and they were even cold and distant, leaving him to weather life's hardships on his own. If they failed to pay attention to him and his emotions, he would be wounded in significant ways. As a result, he would grow into adulthood limited in his ability to give you what you need as his child. He might be incapable of intimacy and relationship; he could have difficulty responding to your emotions and needs, telling you to "toughen up" when you felt sad or alone or afraid. All of this might even result from implicit memories of which he'd have no awareness. Then you, as you became an adult and a parent yourself, would be in danger of passing down the same damaging patterns to your own kids. That's the bad news.

The good news, though—the better-than-good news—is that if you make sense of your experiences and *understand* your father's woundedness and rela-

[BOX CONTINUES ON NEXT PAGE]

tional limitations, you can break the cycle of handing down such pain. You can begin to reflect on those experiences and how they've impacted you.

You might be tempted to simply parent in a way exactly opposite of how your parents did it. But the idea, instead, is to openly reflect on how your experiences with your parents have affected you. You may need to deal with implicit memories that are influencing you without your realizing it. Sometimes it can be helpful to do this work with a therapist, or share your experiences with a friend. However you do it, it's important that you begin getting clear on your own story, because through mirror neurons and implicit memory, we directly pass on our emotional life to our children—for better or for worse. Knowing that our kids live with and through whatever we're experiencing is a powerful insight that can motivate us to begin and continue our journey toward understanding our own stories, the joys as well as the pain. Then we can attune to the needs and signals of our children, creating secure attachment and strong and healthy connection.

Research shows that even adults who experienced less-than-optimal childhoods can parent every bit as effectively, and raise children who feel just as loved and securely attached, as those whose home life was more consistent and loving. It's never too late to begin working on your coherent life narrative, and as you do, your children will reap the rewards.

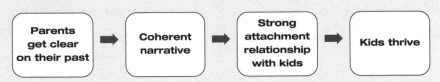

We want to make this point as clearly as possible: early experience is not fate. By making sense of your past you can free yourself from what might otherwise be a cross-generational legacy of pain and insecure attachment, and instead create an inheritance of nurturance and love for your children.

Bringing it All Together

We all have hopes and dreams for our children. For most of us, they involve wanting our kids to be happy, healthy, and fully themselves. Our message throughout this book has been that you can help create this reality for your kids by paying attention during the everyday, ordinary experiences you share with them. That means you can use the obvious teachable moments, but also the difficult challenges and even the humdrum "nothing's really going on" times, as opportunities to prepare your children to be happy and successful, to enjoy good relationships, and to feel content with who they are. In short, to be whole-brain children.

One of the main benefits of the whole-brain perspective, as we've discussed, is that it empowers you to transform the daily parenting challenges that can interrupt the fun and connection you have with your children. Whole-brain parenting allows you to go far beyond mere survival. This approach promotes connection and a deeper understanding between you and your children. An awareness of integration gives you the competence and confidence to handle things in ways that make you closer to your kids, so you can know their minds, and therefore help shape their minds in positive and healthy ways. As a result, not only will your children thrive, but your relationship with them will flourish as well.

So whole-brain parenting isn't just about who your adorable—and at times no doubt exasperating—child is right now, but also about who she will become in the future. It's about integrating her brain, nurturing her mind, and giving her skills that will benefit her as she grows into adolescence and adulthood. By encouraging integration in your children and helping develop their upstairs brain, you prepare them to be better friends, better spouses, and better parents. For example, when a child learns how to SIFT for the sensations, images, feelings, and thoughts in his mind, he'll have a much deeper understanding of himself, and he'll therefore be better able to control himself and connect with others. Likewise, by teaching about connection through conflict, you give your child the invaluable gift of seeing that even unpleasant arguments are opportunities to engage with and learn from the minds of others. Integration is about surviving and thriving, and about your child's well-being now and in the future.

It's extraordinary when you think about the generational impact of the whole-brain approach. Do you realize the power you now have to effect positive change in the future? By giving your children the gift of using their whole brain, you're impacting not just their lives, but also those of the people with whom they interact. Remember mirror neurons and how social the brain is? As we've explained, your child's brain isn't an isolated, "single skull" organ, acting in a vacuum. Self and family and community are fundamentally connected neurologically. Even in our busy, driven, and often isolated lives, we can remember this fundamental reality, that we're all interdependent and connected with one another.

Children who learn this truth have the chance not only to develop happiness and meaning and wisdom in their own lives, but to pass their knowledge along to others as well. When, for example, you help your kids use their internal remote to make their implicit memories explicit, you're helping create within them the skill of self-reflection that will make them much more capable of meaningful interactions with others throughout their lives. The same goes for teaching them about their wheel of awareness. Once they understand about integrating the many parts of themselves, they'll be able to comprehend themselves much more deeply and *actively choose* how they interact with the people around them. They can captain the ship of their lives, more easily avoiding the banks of chaos and rigidity, and more often remaining in the harmonious flow of well-being.

We've found time and again that teaching people about integration and how to apply it in their daily lives has deep and lasting positive effects. For kids, this approach can change the direction of how they develop and set the stage for a life of meaning, kindness, flexibility, and resilience. Some children who have been raised with a whole-brain approach will say things that seem wise beyond their years. A three-year-old we know became so good at identifying and communicating seemingly contradictory emotions that he told his parents, when they returned after he'd spent an evening with his babysitter, "I missed you guys when you were gone, but I also had fun with Katie." And a seven-year-old told her parents on the way to a family picnic, "I've decided not to fuss about my hurt thumb at the park. I'll just tell people I hurt myself, and then have fun and play anyway." This level of self-awareness may seem remarkable in children so young, but it shows you what's possible with the whole-brain approach. When you've become the active author of your life story and not merely the passive scribe of history as it unfolds, you can create a life that you love.

You can see how this kind of self-awareness would lead to healthier relationships down the road, and especially what it could mean for your children's own kids when they become parents. By raising a whole-brain child, you're actually offering your future grandchildren an important gift. For a moment, close your eyes and imagine your child holding his child, and realize the power of what you are passing on. And it won't stop there. Your grandchildren can take what they learn from their parents and pass it further along as a continuing legacy of joy and happiness. Imagine watching your own children connect and redirect with your grandchildren! This is how we integrate our lives across the generations.

We hope this vision will inspire you to become the parent you want to be. Granted, sometimes you'll fall short of your ideals.

And yes, much of what we've shared requires real effort on the part of you and your children. It's not always easy, after all, to go back and retell stories about painful experiences, or to remember to engage the upstairs when your child is upset, rather than triggering the downstairs. But every whole-brain strategy offers practical steps you can take right now to make your life as a family better and more manageable. You don't need to become a perfect superparent or follow some sort of prescribed agenda that programs your kids to be ideal little robot children. You'll still make plenty of mistakes (just as we do), and so will your kids (just as ours do). But the beauty of the whole-brain perspective is that it lets you understand that *even the mistakes are opportunities* to grow and learn. This approach involves being intentional about what we're doing and where we're going, while accepting that we are all human. Intention and attention are our goals, not some rigid, harsh expectation of perfection.

Once you discover the whole-brain approach, you'll likely want to share it with the others in your life who will join you in this great responsibility of raising the future. Whole-brain parents become enthusiastic about sharing what they know with other parents as well as with teachers and caregivers who can work as a team to promote health and well-being in their children. As you create a whole-brain family, you also join a broader vision of creating an entire society full of rich, relational communities where emotional well-being is nurtured for this and future generations. We are all synaptically and socially connected, and bringing integration into our lives creates a world of well-being.

You can see how passionately we believe in the positive impact parents can have on their children and on society as a whole. There's nothing more important you can do as a parent than to be intentional about the way you're shaping your child's mind. What you do matters profoundly.

That being said, don't put too much pressure on yourself. We've emphasized the importance of taking advantage of the moments you have with your kids, but it's not realistic to think you can do this 100 percent of the time. The point is to remain aware of the daily opportunities to nurture your kids' development. But that doesn't mean you have to be constantly talking about the brain or repeatedly prodding your children to recall significant events in their lives. It's just as important to relax and have fun together. And yes, sometimes it's even okay to let a teachable moment pass by.

We realize that all this talk about your power to shape your children's minds and influence the future can feel intimidating at first, especially since genes and experiences affect kids in ways parents simply can't control. But if you really get the concept of *The Whole-Brain Child* at its essence, you'll see that it can liberate you from your fears that you're not doing a good enough job with your kids. It's not your responsibility to avoid all mistakes, any more than you're supposed to remove all obstacles your children face. Instead, your job is to be present with your children and connect with them through the ups and downs of life's journey.

The great news *The Whole-Brain Child* offers is that even the hard times you go through with your kids, even the mistakes you make as you parent, are opportunities to help your children grow, learn, and develop into people who are happy, healthy, and fully themselves. Rather than ignoring their big emotions or distracting them from their struggles, you can nurture their whole brain, *walking with them through these challenges,* staying present and thus strengthening the parent-child bond and helping your kids feel seen, heard, and cared for. We hope what we've shared in these pages will give you the solid foundation and inspiration to create the life you want for your children and your family, now and for the years and generations to come.

REFRIGERATOR SHEET

The Whole-Brain Child
by Daniel J. Siegel and Tina Payne Bryson

INTEGRATING THE LEFT AND RIGHT BRAIN

- **Left + right = clarity and understanding:** Help your kids use both the logical left brain and the emotional right brain as a team.

- **What you can do:**
  - *Connect and redirect:* When your child is upset, connect first emotionally, right brain to right brain. Then, once your child is more in control and receptive, bring in the left-brain lessons and discipline.
  - *Name it to tame it:* When big, right-brain emotions are raging out of control, help your kids tell the story about what's upsetting them, so their left brain can help make sense of their experience and they can feel more in control.

INTEGRATING THE UPSTAIRS BRAIN AND THE DOWNSTAIRS BRAIN

- **Develop the upstairs brain:** Watch for ways to help build the sophisticated upstairs brain, which is "under construction" during childhood and adolescence and can be "hijacked" by the downstairs brain, especially in high-emotion situations.

- **What you can do:**
  - *Engage, don't enrage:* In high-stress situations, engage your child's upstairs brain, rather than triggering the downstairs brain. Don't immediately play the "Because I said so!" card. Instead, ask questions, request alternatives, even negotiate.
  - *Use it or lose it:* Provide lots of opportunities to exercise the upstairs brain. Play "What would you do?" games, and avoid rescuing kids from difficult decisions.
  - *Move it or lose it:* When a child has lost touch with his upstairs brain, help him regain balance by having him move his body.

INTEGRATING MEMORY

- **Make the implicit explicit:** Help your kids make their implicit memories explicit, so that past experiences don't affect them in debilitating ways.

- **What you can do:**
  - *Use the remote of the mind:* When a child is reluctant to narrate a painful event, the internal remote lets her pause, rewind, and fast-forward a story as she tells it, so she can maintain control over how much of it she views.
  - *Remember to remember:* Help your kids exercise their memory by giving them lots of practice at recalling important events: in the car, at the dinner table, wherever.

INTEGRATING THE MANY PARTS OF MYSELF

- **The wheel of awareness:** When your kids get stuck on one particular point on the rim of their wheel of awareness, help them choose where they focus their attention so they can gain more control over how they feel.

- **What you can do:**
  - *Let the clouds of emotion roll by:* Remind kids that feelings come and go; they are temporary states, not enduring traits.
  - *SIFT:* Help your children pay attention to the Sensations, Images, Feelings, and Thoughts within them.
  - *Exercise mindsight:* Mindsight practices teach children to calm themselves and focus their attention where they want.

INTEGRATING SELF AND OTHER

- **Wired for "we":** Watch for ways to capitalize on the brain's built-in capacity for social interaction. Create positive mental models of relationships.

- **What you can do:**
  - *Enjoy each other:* Build fun into the family, so that your kids enjoy positive and satisfying experiences with the people they're with the most.
  - *Connect through conflict:* Instead of an obstacle to avoid, view conflict as an opportunity to teach your kids essential relationship skills, like seeing other people's perspectives, reading nonverbal cues, and making amends.

Whole-Brain Ages and Stages

As your kids get older, you may find yourself wanting help applying the twelve whole-brain strategies to each new age and stage. With that in mind, we've put together the following chart, which you can use as a reference guide anytime you need a quick refresher. Some of what we recommend below will overlap across different ages since the strategies are relevant for different developmental stages. Our goal is to ensure that the book continues to be a vital resource as your child grows and changes, and that you have clear and specific tools at your disposal for each stage of development.

Infant/Toddler (0–3)

TYPE OF INTEGRATION	WHOLE-BRAIN STRATEGY	APPLICATIONS OF THE STRATEGY
Integrating the Left and Right Brain	*#1: Connect and redirect:* When your child is upset, connect first emotionally, right brain to right brain. Then, once she is more in control and receptive, bring in the left-brain lessons and discipline.	Now is the time, as early as possible, to begin teaching your child about emotions. Mirror feelings and use nonverbals (like hugs and empathetic facial expressions) to show that you understand: *You're frustrated, aren't you?* Then, once you've connected, set the boundary: *Biting hurts. Please be gentle.* Finally, focus on an appropriate alternative or move on to something else: *Hey, there's your bear. I haven't seen him in a long time.*
	#2: Name it to tame it: When big, right-brain emotions are raging out of control, help your child tell the story about what's upsetting him. In doing so, he'll use his left brain to make sense of his experience and feel more in control.	Even at this young age, make it a habit to acknowledge and name feelings: *You look so sad. That really hurt, didn't it?* Then tell the story. With small children, you'll need to be the primary narrator. Use your words and even act out the fall or the bump, possibly using humor, and watch your child's fascination. It can be helpful to make a homemade book with pictures or photos to retell an upsetting story, or to prepare your child for a transition, like a new bedtime routine or starting preschool.
Integrating the Upstairs and Downstairs	*#3: Engage, don't enrage:* In high-stress situations, engage your child's upstairs brain by asking her to consider and plan and choose, rather than triggering her downstairs brain, which is less about thinking and more about reacting.	Nobody likes to be told no, and it's an especially ineffective strategy to use too often with toddlers. When possible, avoid outright power struggles with your little one. Save your no for when you really need it. The next time you hear yourself beginning to forbid her from hitting the mirror with the stick, stop. Instead, engage her upstairs brain: *Let's go outside. What could you do with that stick in the yard?*
	#4: Use it or lose it: Provide lots of opportunities to exercise the upstairs brain so it can be strong and integrated with the downstairs brain and the body.	As often as possible, find ways to let your child use her upstairs brain and make decisions for herself. *Do you want to wear your blue or red shirt today? Would you like milk or water with dinner?* When you read together, ask brain-growing questions: *How do you think the kitty will get down from the tree? Why does the girl look sad?*

TYPE OF INTEGRATION	WHOLE-BRAIN STRATEGY	APPLICATIONS OF THE STRATEGY
Integrating the Upstairs and Downstairs	*#5: Move it or lose it:* A powerful way to help a child regain upstairs-downstairs balance is to have him move his body.	When your child is upset, make sure to acknowledge his feelings. This should always be your first move. But then, as quickly as possible, get him moving. Roughhouse with him. Play follow the leader. Race him to his bedroom and back. Get him to move and you'll change his mood.
Integrating Memory	*#6: Use the remote of the mind:* After an upsetting event, the internal remote lets a child pause, rewind, and fast-forward a story as she tells it, so she can maintain control over how much of it she views.	Children this small may not know about a remote, but they know the power of a story. Enjoy this time when your child wants to tell (and retell) stories. Rather than pausing and fast-forwarding, you may end up simply pressing play repeatedly as you tell the same story multiple times. Even if you feel annoyed at having to go over the account again and again, remember that storytelling produces understanding, healing, and integration.
	#7: Remember to remember: Help your kids exercise their memory by giving them lots of practice at remembering.	At this age, ask simple questions, focusing on returning your child's attention to the details of her day. *We went to Carrie's house today, didn't we? And do you remember what we did there?* Questions like these are the building blocks for an integrated memory system.
Integrating the Many Parts of Myself	*#8: Let the clouds of emotion roll by:* Remind kids that feelings come and go. Fear, frustration, and loneliness are temporary states, not enduring traits.	Lay the foundation for an awareness of the difference between "feel" and "am." When young children feel sad (or angry or afraid), they have a hard time understanding that they won't always feel that way. So help them say, "I *feel* sad right now, but I know I'll be happy later." Be careful, though, that you don't dismiss the actual feelings. Acknowledge the present emotion and provide comfort, then help your child understand that he won't feel sad forever, that he will feel better soon.

TYPE OF INTEGRATION	WHOLE-BRAIN STRATEGY	APPLICATIONS OF THE STRATEGY
Integrating the Many Parts of Myself	*#9: SIFT:* Help your children notice and understand the sensations, images, feelings, and thoughts within them.	Help your child become aware of and talk about her internal world. Ask questions that guide her toward noticing bodily sensations (*Are you hungry?*), mental images (*What do you picture when you think about Grandma's house?*), feelings (*It's frustrating when the blocks fall, isn't it?*), and thoughts (*What do you think will happen when Jill comes over tomorrow?*).
	#10: Exercise mindsight: Mindsight practices teach children to calm themselves and focus their attention where they want.	Even small children can learn to be still and take calm breaths, if only for a few seconds. Have your child lie on her back and place a toy boat on her stomach. Show her how to take slow, big breaths to make the boat go up and down. Keep this exercise very short since she's so young. Just let her experience the feeling of being still, quiet, and peaceful.
Integrating Self and Other	*#11: Increase the family fun factor:* Build fun into the family, so that your kids enjoy positive and satisfying experiences with the people they're with the most.	Follow your child's lead and just play. Tickle him, laugh with him, love him. Stack things up, knock them down. Bang on pots and pans, go to the park, roll the ball. With every interaction in which you focus on and attune to your child, you can create positive expectations in his mind about what it means to love and be in a relationship.
	#12: Connect through conflict: Rather than an obstacle to avoid, view conflict as an opportunity to teach your kids essential relationship skills.	Talk with your child about sharing and taking turns, but don't expect too much from her. In the coming years you will have many opportunities to teach social skills and discipline. Right now, if there's conflict between her and another child, help her express how she feels and how the other child might feel, and help them problem-solve if possible. Then redirect them both so they can transition into a different activity they can each enjoy.

Preschooler (3–6)

TYPE OF INTEGRATION	WHOLE-BRAIN STRATEGY	APPLICATIONS OF THE STRATEGY
Integrating the Left and Right Brain	*#1: Connect and redirect:* When your child is upset, connect first emotionally, right brain to right brain. Then, once she is more in control and receptive, bring in the left-brain lessons and discipline.	First, lovingly hear what's upset your child. Hug her and repeat back to her what you've heard with nurturing nonverbal communication: *You're really disappointed that Molly can't come over?* Then, once you've connected, help direct her toward problem solving and more appropriate behavior: *I know you're upset, but you need to be gentle with Mommy. Do you have another idea for playing? Maybe we could see if Molly can come over tomorrow.*
	#2: Name it to tame it: When big, right-brain emotions are raging out of control, help your child tell the story about what's upsetting him. In doing so, he'll use his left brain to make sense of his experience and feel more in control.	Whether it's a "small-t" or "big-T" trauma, you can start the storytelling process almost right away (once you've connected right brain to right). At this age, he'll need you to take the lead: *You know what I saw? I saw you running, and when your foot hit that slippery spot, you fell. Is that what happened?* If he continues the story, great. But if needed, you can continue: *So then you started crying, and I ran over to you and . . .* It can be helpful to make a homemade book with drawings or photos to retell an upsetting story, or to prepare your child for a transition, like a new bedtime routine or starting school.
Integrating the Upstairs and Downstairs	*#3: Engage, don't enrage:* In high-stress situations, engage your child's upstairs brain by asking her to consider and plan and choose, rather than triggering her downstairs brain, which is less about thinking and more about reacting.	Setting clear boundaries is important, but we often say no more than we need to. When your child is upset, be creative. Instead of saying, *We don't act that way,* ask, *What's another way you could handle that?* Instead of *I don't like the way you're talking,* try, *Can you think of another way to say that, one that will be more polite?* Then praise her when she uses her upstairs brain to come up with alternatives. A great question to help avoid power struggles is, *Can you come up with an idea for how we can* both *get what we want?*

TYPE OF INTEGRATION	WHOLE-BRAIN STRATEGY	APPLICATIONS OF THE STRATEGY
Integrating the Upstairs and Downstairs	*#4: Use it or lose it:* Provide lots of opportunities to exercise the upstairs brain so it can be strong and integrated with the downstairs brain and the body.	In addition to introducing your child to shapes and letters and numbers, play "What would you do?" games that present him with hypothetical dilemmas. *What would you do if you were at the park and found a toy that you really wanted, but you knew it belonged to someone else?* Read together and ask your child to predict how the story will end. Also, give him lots of opportunities to make decisions for himself, even (and especially) when it's difficult.
	#5: Move it or lose it: A powerful way to help a child regain upstairs-downstairs balance is to have him move his body.	Kids this age love to move. So when your child is upset, and after you've acknowledged his feelings, give him reasons to move his body. Wrestle with him. Play "keep it up" with a balloon. Toss a ball back and forth while he's telling you why he's upset. Moving the body is a powerful way to change a mood.
Integrating Memory	*#6: Use the remote of the mind:* After an upsetting event, the internal remote lets a child pause, rewind, and fast-forward a story as she tells it, so she can maintain control over how much of it she views.	Most likely, your preschooler loves telling stories. Encourage this. Tell stories about anything that happens: good, bad, and in between. And when a significant event occurs, be willing to narrate and renarrate the story. Even if your child may not know much about remote controls, she may be able to "go back" and "pause" her story. She'll be delighted to hear you tell, and help you tell and retell, the story of any big moment in her life. So be prepared to "press play" over and over again—and know that when you do, you're promoting healing and integration.

TYPE OF INTEGRATION	WHOLE-BRAIN STRATEGY	APPLICATIONS OF THE STRATEGY
Integrating Memory	*#7: Remember to remember:* Help your kids exercise their memory by giving them lots of practice at remembering.	Ask questions that exercise the memory: *What did Ms. Alvarez think of the robot you took in for sharing today? Remember when Uncle Chris took you to get a snow cone?* Play memory games that ask your child to match up pairs or find like items, maybe pictures of friends and family with specific stories or memories. Especially on important events you want him to remember, take turns talking about the details that stood out for each of you.
Integrating the Many Parts of Myself	*#8: Let the clouds of emotion roll by:* Remind kids that feelings come and go. Fear, frustration, and loneliness are temporary states, not enduring traits.	One reason big feelings can be so uncomfortable for small children is that they don't view those emotions as temporary. So while you comfort your child when she's upset, teach her that feelings come and go. Help her see that it's good to acknowledge her emotions, but it's also good to realize that even though she's sad (or angry or scared) right now, she'll probably be happy again in a few minutes. You can even "lead the witness" and ask, *When do you think you'll feel better?*
	#9: SIFT: Help your children notice and understand the sensations, images, feelings, and thoughts within them.	Talk to your child about his inner world. Help him understand that he can notice and talk about what's going on in his mind and body. He probably won't be ready for the acronym SIFT yet, but you can help him ask questions that guide him toward noticing bodily sensations (*Are you hungry?*), mental images (*What do you picture when you think about Grandma's house?*), feelings (*It's frustrating when friends don't share, isn't it?*), and thoughts (*What do you think will happen at school tomorrow?*).

TYPE OF INTEGRATION	WHOLE-BRAIN STRATEGY	APPLICATIONS OF THE STRATEGY
Integrating the Many Parts of Myself	*#10: Exercise mindsight:* Mindsight practices teach children to calm themselves and focus their attention where they want.	At this age, kids can practice taking calm breaths, especially if you keep the exercises brief. Have your child lie on her back, and place a toy boat on her stomach. Show her how to take slow big breaths to make the boat go up and down. You can also tap into your child's vivid imagination at this age to give her practice focusing attention and shifting her emotional state: *Imagine that you are resting on the warm sand at the beach and you are feeling calm and happy.*
Integrating Self and Other	*#11: Increase the family fun factor:* Build fun into the family, so that your kids enjoy positive and satisfying experiences with the people they're with the most.	You don't have to try too hard to have fun with your preschooler. Just being with you is paradise for him. Spend time with him, play games, and laugh together. Facilitate fun with siblings and grandparents. Be silly and turn potential power struggles into playful and funny moments of joining. When you are intentional about having fun and creating enjoyable family rituals, you're making an investment in your relationship that will pay off for years to come.
	#12: Connect through conflict: Rather than an obstacle to avoid, view conflict as an opportunity to teach your kids essential relationship skills.	Use conflict your preschooler faces—with her siblings, with her classmates, even with you—to teach her lessons about how to get along with others. Sharing, taking turns, and asking for and granting forgiveness are important concepts she's ready to learn. Model these for her, and take the time to kneel down and help her understand what it means to be in a relationship and how to be considerate and respectful of others, even during times of conflict.

Early School Age (6–9)

TYPE OF INTEGRATION	WHOLE-BRAIN STRATEGY	APPLICATIONS OF THE STRATEGY
Integrating the Left and Right Brain	*#1: Connect and redirect:* When your child is upset, connect first emotionally, right brain to right brain. Then, once she is more in control and receptive, bring in the left-brain lessons and discipline.	Listen first, then repeat how your child is feeling. At the same time, use your nonverbal communication to comfort. Hugs and physical touch, along with empathetic facial expressions, remain powerful tools for calming big emotions. Then redirect through problem solving and, depending on the circumstance, discipline and boundary setting.
	#2: Name it to tame it: When big, right-brain emotions are raging out of control, help your child tell the story about what's upsetting him. In doing so, he'll use his left brain to make sense of his experience and feel more in control.	Whether it's a "small-t" or "big-T" trauma, you can start the storytelling process almost right away (once you've connected right brain to right brain). Whereas with younger kids you may need to do most of the storytelling and with older kids you can let them take the lead, with a school-age child you need to balance the two. Ask lots of questions: *Did you just not notice that the swing was coming toward you?* or *What did your teacher do when he said that to you? What happened after that?* It can be helpful to make a homemade book with drawings or photos to retell an upsetting story, or to prepare your child for something she is dreading, like a visit to the dentist or a move.
Integrating the Upstairs and Downstairs	*#3: Engage, don't enrage:* In high-stress situations, engage your child's upstairs brain by asking her to consider and plan and choose, rather than triggering her downstairs brain, which is less about thinking and more about reacting.	As always, connect first. Avoid immediately playing the "Because I said so!" card. Your child's upstairs brain is blossoming right now, so let it do its job. Explain your reasons, invite questions, ask for alternative solutions, and even negotiate. You're the authority in the relationship, and there's no place for disrespect, but you can encourage your child to come up with different approaches to discipline or learning a lesson. When we expect and facilitate more sophisticated thinking, we're less likely to get a reactive, fighting response.

TYPE OF INTEGRATION	WHOLE-BRAIN STRATEGY	APPLICATIONS OF THE STRATEGY
Integrating the Upstairs and Downstairs	*#4: Use it or lose it:* Provide lots of opportunities to exercise the upstairs brain so it can be strong and integrated with the downstairs brain and the body.	Play "What would you do?" games and present your child with dilemmas: *If a bully was picking on someone at school and there were no adults around, what would you do?* Encourage empathy and self-understanding through reflective dialogues about how others feel, and about his own intentions, desires, and beliefs. Also, let your child struggle with difficult decisions and situations. Whenever you can do so responsibly, avoid solving and resist rescuing, even when he makes minor mistakes or not-so-great choices. After all, your goal here isn't perfection on every decision right now, but an optimally developed upstairs brain down the road.
	#5: Move it or lose it: A powerful way to help a child regain upstairs-downstairs balance is to have him move his body.	Connect with your child when she's upset, then find ways to get her moving. Get on your bikes together. Play "keep it up" with a balloon or try some yoga poses. Depending on your particular child, you may need to be more direct about what you're doing. Don't feel that you need to "trick" her or hide your strategy. Be direct and explain to her the "move it or lose it" concept, then use the lesson to teach her that we can actually control our moods to a significant extent.
Integrating Memory	*#6: Use the remote of the mind:* After a painful event, the internal remote lets a child pause, rewind, and fast-forward a story as she tells it, so she can maintain control over how much of it she views.	A child this age may shy away from retelling difficult stories or recalling painful memories. Help him understand the importance of looking at what's happened to him. Be gentle and nurturing, and give him the power to pause the story at any point, and even to fast-forward past unpleasant details. But make sure that at some point, even if it's later on, you rewind and tell the entire story, including even the painful parts.

TYPE OF INTEGRATION	WHOLE-BRAIN STRATEGY	APPLICATIONS OF THE STRATEGY
Integrating Memory	*#7: Remember to remember:* Help your kids exercise their memory by giving them lots of practice at remembering.	In the car, at the dinner table, wherever, help your child talk about her experiences, so she can integrate her implicit and explicit memories. This is especially important when it comes to the most important moments of her life, like family experiences, important friendships, and rites of passage. Simply by asking questions and encouraging recollection, you can help her remember and understand important events from the past, which will help her better understand what's happening to her in the present.
Integrating the Many Parts of Myself	*#8: Let the clouds of emotion roll by:* Remind kids that feelings come and go. Fear, frustration, and loneliness are temporary states, not enduring traits.	Help your child pay attention to the words he uses when he talks about his feelings. There's nothing wrong with saying, "I'm scared." But help him understand that another way to say it is, "I *feel* scared." This minor shift in vocabulary can help him understand the subtle but important distinction between "feel" and "am." He may feel afraid in the moment, but that experience is temporary, not permanent. To give him perspective, ask him how he expects to feel in five minutes, five hours, five days, five months, and five years.
	#9: SIFT: Help your children notice and understand the sensations, images, feelings, and thoughts within them.	Introduce the wheel of awareness. Also, play the SIFT game in the car or at dinner and actually teach your child the acronym. Help her understand that we need to notice what's going on within ourselves if we want to control the way we feel and act. Ask questions that guide her toward noticing bodily sensations (*Are you hungry?*), mental images (*What do you picture when you think about Grandma's house?*), feelings (*It's not fun to feel left out, is it?*), and thoughts (*What do you think will happen at school tomorrow?*).

TYPE OF INTEGRATION	WHOLE-BRAIN STRATEGY	APPLICATIONS OF THE STRATEGY
Integrating the Many Parts of Myself	*#10: Exercise mindsight:* Mindsight practices teach children to calm themselves and focus their attention where they want.	Children this age can understand and feel the benefits of getting calm and focusing the mind. Give them practice at being still and quiet, and let them enjoy the calm within. By guiding their mind through visualization and imagination, show them that they have the ability to focus their attention on thoughts and feelings that bring them happiness and peace. Show them that anytime they need to calm themselves, they can simply slow down and pay attention to their breathing.
Integrating Self and Other	*#11: Increase the family fun factor:* Build fun into the family, so your kids enjoy positive and satisfying experiences with the people they're with the most.	Do what you love doing together. Have a family movie night with popcorn. Play a board game. Ride bikes. Make up a story together. Sing and dance. Just spend time together being happy and silly, and it will create a strong relational foundation for the future. Be intentional about having fun and creating enjoyable rituals and memories.
	#12: Connect through conflict: Rather than an obstacle to avoid, view conflict as an opportunity to teach your kids essential relationship skills.	Your child is old enough now for more relational sophistication. Explicitly teach a skill, then practice it. Explain about seeing other people's perspectives, then pick out random people in a store or restaurant and try to guess what's important to them and where they're coming from. Teach about reading nonverbal cues, then play a game to see how many examples (frowning, shrugging, lifting eyebrows, etc.) you can come up with. Teach about going beyond apologizing when we've messed up, then come up with a timely example where your child can put it into practice by writing a letter or replacing something important.

Later School Age (9–12)

TYPE OF INTEGRATION	WHOLE-BRAIN STRATEGY	APPLICATIONS OF THE STRATEGY
Integrating the Left and Right Brain	*#1: Connect and Redirect:* When your child is upset, connect first emotionally, right brain to right brain. Then, once she is more in control and receptive, bring in the left-brain lessons and discipline.	Listen first, then reflect back how your child is feeling. Be careful not to condescend or talk down to her. Just echo what you hear. And use nonverbals. Even though your child is growing up, she still wants to be nurtured by you. Once she feels felt, it's time to redirect to planning and, if necessary, discipline. Show your child the respect of speaking clearly and directly. She's old enough to hear and understand a logical explanation of the situation and any resulting consequences.
	#2: Name it to tame it: When big, right-brain emotions are raging out of control, help your child tell the story about what's upsetting him. In doing so, he'll use his left brain to make sense of his experience and feel more in control.	First, acknowledge feelings. This is no less true for a big kid than it is for a small one (or an adult). Just express, explicitly, what you observe: *I don't blame you for being upset. I would be, too.* Then facilitate the storytelling. Ask questions and be present, but let him tell his own story, in his own time. Especially in painful moments, it's important that kids talk about what's happened to them. But we can't force them to do so. We can only be patient and present and allow them to talk when they're ready. If your child doesn't want to talk to you about it, suggest journaling, or help him find someone he will talk to.
Integrating the Upstairs and Downstairs	*#3: Engage, don't enrage:* In high-stress situations, engage your child's upstairs brain by asking her to consider and plan and choose, rather than triggering her downstairs brain, which is less about thinking and more about reacting.	This is one of the worst ages to play the "Because I said so!" card. Instead, encourage your child's blossoming upstairs brain by appealing to it whenever you can. Maintain your authority in the relationship, but as much as possible, discuss alternatives and negotiate with her when it comes to rules and discipline. Be respectful and creative as you help her improve her higher-order thinking faculties by asking her to participate with you in making decisions and coming up with solutions.

TYPE OF INTEGRATION	WHOLE-BRAIN STRATEGY	APPLICATIONS OF THE STRATEGY
Integrating the Upstairs and Downstairs	*#4: Use it or lose it:* Provide lots of opportunities to exercise the upstairs brain so it can be strong and integrated with the downstairs brain and the body.	Hypothetical situations become more and more fun as a child's brain develops. Play "What would you do?" games and present your child with dilemmas. These games can be purchased, but you can come up with your own situations: *If your friend's mother had been drinking before she was supposed to drive you home, how would you handle it?* Encourage empathy and self-understanding through reflective dialogues about how others feel, and your child's own intentions, desires, and beliefs. Also, let him struggle with difficult decisions and situations, even when he makes minor mistakes or not-so-great choices. After all, your goal here isn't perfection on every decision right now, but an optimally developed upstairs brain down the road.
	#5: Move it or lose it: A powerful way to help a child regain upstairs-downstairs balance is to have him move his body.	Be direct about how moving his body can help shift your child's mood. Especially when he's upset, explain how helpful it is to take a break and get up and move. Suggest a bike ride or a walk, or do something physically active with him, such as playing Ping-Pong. Even taking a break to stretch or play with a yo-yo can help.
Integrating Memory	*#6: Use the remote of the mind:* After a painful event, the internal remote lets a child pause, rewind, and fast-forward a story as she tells it, so she can maintain control over how much of it she views.	As she approaches adolescence, your child may become more reluctant to talk with you about painful experiences. Explain the importance of implicit memory, and how the associations of a past experience can still affect her. Teach her that she can gain control over an experience by retelling the story. Be gentle and nurturing, and give her the power to pause the story at any point, and even to fast-forward past unpleasant details. But make sure that at some point, even if it's later on, you rewind and tell the entire story, including the painful parts.

TYPE OF INTEGRATION	WHOLE-BRAIN STRATEGY	APPLICATIONS OF THE STRATEGY
Integrating Memory	*#7: Remember to remember:* Help your kids exercise their memory by giving them lots of practice at remembering.	In the car and at the dinner table, in scrapbooks or journals, help your child think about her experiences, so she can integrate her implicit and explicit memories. This is especially important when it comes to the most important moments of her life, like family experiences, important friendships, and rites of passage. Simply by asking questions and encouraging recollection, you can help her remember and understand important events from the past, which will help her better understand what's happening to her in the present.
Integrating the Many Parts of Myself	*#8: Let the clouds of emotion roll by:* Remind kids that feelings come and go. Fear, frustration, and loneliness are temporary states, not enduring traits.	Your child is old enough to understand this point on a conscious level, but be sure to hear his feelings before you teach this information. Then, once you've validated his feelings, help him understand that they won't last forever. Highlight the subtle but important distinction between "I *feel* sad" and "I *am* sad." To give him perspective, ask him how he expects to feel in five minutes, five hours, five days, five months, and five years.
	#9: SIFT: Help your children notice and understand the sensations, images, feelings, and thoughts within them.	Some kids this age may actually be interested in the concept of SIFTing to see what's going on inside themselves. Understanding these categories can give them some measure of control over their lives, which, as they move toward being teenagers, will increasingly feel more and more chaotic. Also, this is a great age to regularly use the wheel of awareness to help understand and respond to issues that arise.

TYPE OF INTEGRATION	WHOLE-BRAIN STRATEGY	APPLICATIONS OF THE STRATEGY
Integrating the Many Parts of Myself	*#10: Exercise mindsight:* Mindsight practices teach children to calm themselves and focus their attention where they want.	Explain to your child the significant benefits of getting calm and focusing the mind. Give her practice at being still and quiet, and let her enjoy the calm within. Show her that she has the ability to focus her attention on thoughts and feelings that bring her happiness and peace. Introduce her to some of the practices in this book, such as guided visualizations and focusing on her breath, or look at some of the infinite resources you'll find at the library or online.
Integrating Self and Other	*#11: Increase the family fun factor:* Build fun into the family, so that your kids enjoy positive and satisfying experiences with the people they're with the most.	The cliché is that as kids move toward their teenage years, they less and less enjoy being with their parents. To some extent this is true. But the more meaningful and enjoyable experiences you give your child now, the more he'll want to be with you in the years to come. Kids this age still love silliness and play, so don't underestimate the power of a game of charades or an interactive board game when it comes to strengthening family relationships. Go camping. Cook together. Visit a theme park. Just find ways to appreciate being together, creating fun rituals you can enjoy for years to come.
	#12: Connect through conflict: Rather than an obstacle to avoid, view conflict as an opportunity to teach your kids essential relationship skills.	All the relational and conflict resolution skills you've been trying to give your child since she was learning to talk—seeing other people's perspectives, reading nonverbal cues, sharing, apologizing—are the same lessons you're teaching as she moves toward adolescence. Keep talking about these skills explicitly, and practice them. Whether you're asking your child to see the world through someone else's eyes, or write a note of apology, teach her that conflict is something not to avoid but to resolve, and that doing so often improves a relationship.

Acknowledgments

Being parents and therapists ourselves, we know the importance of finding applications that are simple, accessible, practical, and effective. At the same time, we are both trained as scientists, so we know the power of scientifically grounded work that builds on cutting-edge knowledge. We are profoundly grateful to the many people who have helped us keep this book based firmly on scientific research, but also solidly planted in the practical world of everyday parenting.

We have been fortunate to work with academic and professional colleagues at both USC and UCLA in various departments who both supported our work and inspired us with their research endeavors into the brain and relationships. Dan's first book, *The Developing Mind*, was revised during the time we wrote *The Whole-Brain Child*, with the incorporation of over two thousand new scientific references. We want to thank the scientists and researchers whose work we drew on so we could ensure that the translation of this knowledge is as current as possible.

The manuscript itself emerged in close collaboration with our wonderful literary agent and friend, Doug Abrams, who lent his novelist's eye and editor's hands to mold the book throughout its gestation. It has been a pleasure to work like three whole-brain musketeers taking on the challenges of translating such important ideas into direct, accessible, and accurate applications of the science for everyday use. We can't wait for our next adventure together!

We also thank our clinical colleagues and the students at the Mindsight Institute and in our various seminars and parenting groups (especially the Tuesday night and Monday morning groups) who have provided feedback about many of the ideas that make up the foundation of the whole-brain approach to parenting. A number of individuals read the manuscript and contributed valuable comments that helped "field-test" the book. Laura Hubber, Jenny Lorant, Lisa Rosenberg, Ellen Main, Jay Bryson, Sara Smirin, Jeff Newell, Gina Griswold, Celeste Neuhoff, Elisa Nixon, Christine Adams, Sarah Heidel, Lea Payne, Heather Sourial, Bradley Whitford, and Andre van Rooyen offered excellent feedback on the text, illustrations, and cover. Others were essential to this book's creation, and we especially thank Deborah and Galen Buckwalter, Jen and Chris Williams, Liz and Steve Olson, Linda Burrow, Robert Colegrove, Patti Ni, and Gordon Walker for their support and time.

We gratefully acknowledge the efforts of Beth Rashbaum, our original editor, as well as our current editor, Marnie Cochran, whose dedication and wisdom (not to mention patience) guided us in every stage of the process. We were fortunate to have two editors who care profoundly for books and for children. And we offer a big, artistic thank-you to our illustrator, Merrilee Liddiard, a delight to work with, who lent her talent, creative eye, and experience as a mom to making the book a whole-brain experience for the reader.

To the parents and teachers who have heard us speak or whom we've had the privilege of working with in some capacity, we are deeply thankful for the enthusiasm with which you've embraced the whole-brain perspective. Your stories of how these approaches have transformed your relationships with your children have inspired us throughout this process. We particularly thank all the parents and patients whose stories and experiences inform this book.

Although we've changed your names and the details of your stories here, *we* know who you are, and we're grateful. Thanks, also, to all of you who discussed and voted on possible book titles while watching Little League games and enjoying Lily's fourth birthday party next door! It certainly has been a community endeavor to bring these practical ideas into as clear and concise an expression as possible.

Our devotion to helping children develop resilient minds and compassionate relationships begins at home. We are profoundly grateful not only to our own parents, but to our spouses, Caroline and Scott, whose wisdom and direct editorial input are woven throughout these pages. Our spouses are not only our best friends but also our best collaborators, and they helped us through countless drafts of writing and rewriting, sharing their own literary talents and parenting wisdom. This book could not have happened without them. Scott generously lent his English professor's eye, writer's mind, and editor's pen to make this book flow and read more clearly. This family effort is expressed most fully in our own personal lives through our children, our best teachers, whose love and playfulness, emotion and devotion, are inspiring to us in ways words cannot begin to describe. We thank them from the depths of our hearts for the opportunity to be their parents along this life journey. It is their exploration of the many dimensions of their development that gives us the motivation to share these ideas about integration with you. So it is to our children that we lovingly dedicate *The Whole-Brain Child* in hopes that this book will also allow you and the children you care for to share the journey toward integration, health, and well-being.

Index

DANIEL J. SIEGEL, M.D., is a graduate of Harvard Medical School and completed his postgraduate medical education at UCLA with training in pediatrics and child, adolescent, and adult psychiatry. He is currently a clinical professor of psychiatry at the UCLA School of Medicine, co-director of UCLA's Mindful Awareness Research Center, co-investigator at the Center for Culture, Brain and Development, and executive director of the Mindsight Institute, an educational center devoted to promoting insight, compassion, and empathy in individuals, families, institutions, and communities. Dr. Siegel's psychotherapy practice over the last twenty-five years has included children, adolescents, adults, couples, and families. Dr. Siegel is also the author of several acclaimed books, including *Parenting from the Inside Out: How a Deeper Self-Understanding Can Help You Raise Children Who Thrive* (with Mary Hartzell, M.Ed.), *The Mindful Brain, Mindsight: The New Science of Personal Transformation,* and *The Developing Mind.* He lives in Los Angeles with his wife and two children. For more information about his educational programs and resources, please visit drdansiegel.com.

TINA PAYNE BRYSON, PH.D., is a psychotherapist at Pediatric and Adolescent Psychology Associates in Arcadia, California, where she sees children and adolescents, as well as provides parenting consultations. In addition to writing and lecturing to parents, educators, and professionals, she serves as the director of parenting education and development for the Mindsight Institute, focusing on how to understand relationships in the context of the developing brain. Dr. Bryson earned her Ph.D. from the University of Southern California, where her research explored attachment science, child-rearing theory, and the emerging field of interpersonal neurobiology. She lives near Los Angeles with her husband and three children. For more information about her work and parenting resources, please visit tinabryson.com.